PADDLE STEAMERS

Blandford Press
Poole   Dorset

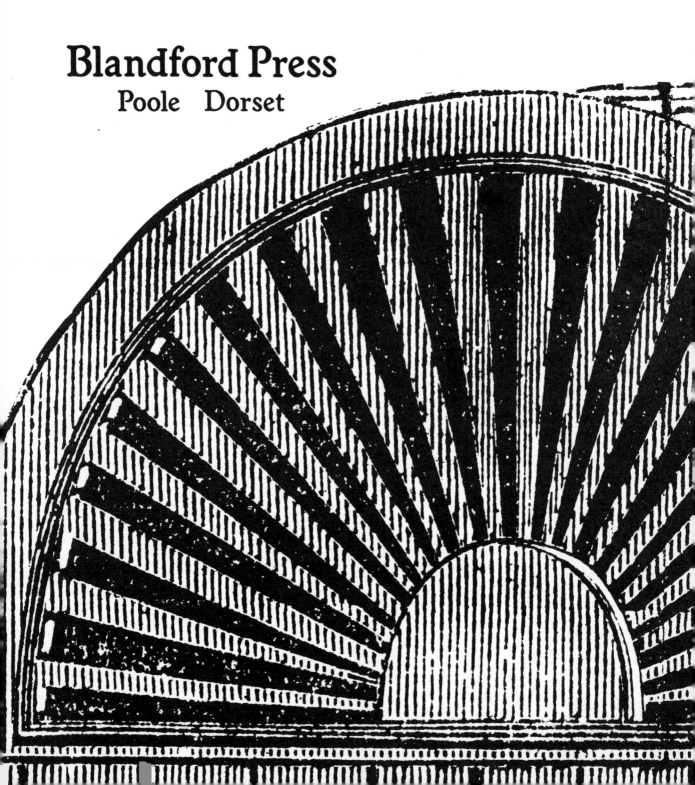

PADDLE STEAMERS

Bernard Cox

To Diana
Who was born too late to witness
the hey-day of the paddle steamer

First published in Great Britain
by Blandford Press Ltd, Link House,
West Street, Poole, Dorset BH15 1LL

Cox, Bernard
Paddle steamers.
1. Paddle steamers – History
I. Title
387.2'43   HE566.P3

ISBN 0-7137-0924-3

Phototypeset by Oliver Burridge & Co. Ltd
Printed in Great Britain by Fletcher & Son Ltd, Norwich
Books bound by Richard Clay (Chaucer Press) Ltd, Bungay, Suffolk
Designed by
Origination, Bournemouth

Contents

Foreword

The part that paddle-propelled vessels have played in maritime history is considerable. They are probably best remembered in their rôle as excursion steamers which for over 150 years have threshed their way through sea, river and lake, bringing to their millions of passengers a day of enjoyment or at worst the first uncomfortable signs of sea-sickness. Yet the paddle steamer has undertaken many more important jobs, from the thousand-mile voyages of exploration and discovery, coupled with ease of communication to villages and trading posts in America and Australia, to the more graceful task of a Royal Yacht. Nor must their contribution to towing and salvage, especially in the 19th century, be forgotten when many a sailing ship skipper becalmed offshore has welcomed a plume of smoke and the steady beat of paddles.

Millions of commuters have been served by paddle ferries gently splashing their way with snowy wake across river or estuary, carrying them to their place of work or residence. The paddler has been (and still is) an attraction in many tourist spots of Europe, offering unrivalled scenic views unobtainable from car or train, whilst stories of the great American river boat races will be handed down from generation to generation. The wartime tasks of vessels designed for far different purposes has been varied and often difficult.

And now the days of the paddler are numbered. More modern forms of propulsion have taken their place, or routes have been abandoned because of lack of patronage due to the motor car or the aeroplane. The hovercraft and hydrofoil now have their devotees, but the stately progress of a paddle steamer with its wake of creamy wash and plume of smoke emitting from a tall stately funnel will linger on in the memories of those who have watched the paddle steamer at work.

Not that the paddler is completely gone, for the work of museums and preservation societies must not be forgotten and in many corners of the world there are relics of the day when steam and feathering floats were supreme. Although many of these steamers are no longer operational, they serve as a reminder of a chapter of maritime history which I hope I have outlined in this book.

This work has not set out to be a definitive history of the paddle steamer, be it side- or stern-wheeler, but the text and photographs which follow are an attempt to outline and show the reader the many uses to which the paddle steamer has been put. Many of the photographs have been taken from my own collection which has been built up over a period of a quarter of a century. Many of the steamers, such as Brunel's *Great Western*, are well known and have in fact been the subject of many volumes outlining in full their outstanding contribution to the history of transport on water. Others, such as the United States Corps of Transport's paddler *Mississippi* are perhaps chronicled for the first time. I have attempted to present a general cross-section of paddlers, known and unknown, in the hope that the reader will seek further information on this disappearing type of vessel.

1 The Development of the Paddle Steamer

It is of course futile to search further back than the invention of the steam engine to seek representative samples of a paddle steamer, which by definition must possess some form of reciprocating engine. Nevertheless in this work I have included vessels which broadly follow the design and purpose of the traditional paddler, yet are not steamers within the full meaning of the word, in order to present a more general profile of ships fitted with the revolving wheel.

The first recorded example of a paddle wheel used for propulsion of a waterborne vessel dates back to Roman times when galleys, in which oxen were harnessed to a type of treadmill, gave motion to revolving wheels attached to the side of the ship, which propelled and moved the ship in calm waters. The great disadvantage was that, in heavy seas, the unfortunate animals were unable to stand to provide the motive power when it was most needed. Neither were any great variations in speed easily obtained and it would appear that the Romans gave little attention to any further development of this means of travel.

In the 7th century the Chinese had vessels worked by men turning cranks inside the ship in much the same way as hand-propelled boats found on children's boating lakes today.

It is generally acknowledged that it was the efforts of the British engineer, William Symington, sponsored by Lord Dundas, that led to the first successful trials of a paddle-propelled steamship, the *Charlotte Dundas* on the Forth and Clyde Canal on a windy and blustery day in March 1802.

Before that, however, several less favourable attempts at paddle propulsion had been made dating back to 1543 when a Spaniard, Blasco de Garay, fitted paddle wheels to a ship named *Trinidad* which, it was reported, reached a speed of four knots. Despite the fact that eyewitnesses had reported clouds of steam emitting from the vessel, it would appear that this was from a cauldron of hot water on the deck and that the paddle wheels had been set into motion by the combined efforts of some fifty men! One wonders if perhaps the 'clouds of steam' were occasioned by the perspiration of the motive crew.

In 1709 a Frenchman, Denis Papin, fitted a boat with steam-powered paddles intending a voyage from Marburg to London. His efforts were of no avail as the watermen of the River Fielda had grave suspicions about his vessel and it was sabotaged before the voyage took place. A further attempt by Papin during the following year also came to naught, despite the submission of documents to the Royal Society in London.

The first patent for a steamboat was issued in 1736 to Jonathan Hulls of Gloucestershire, England, on behalf of a vessel which was to be used 'for towing ships and vessels out of, or into, any harbour or river, against wind or tide, or in a calm'. Hulls appears to have met with unsurmountable problems and what might have been the first paddle-driven tug was never built.

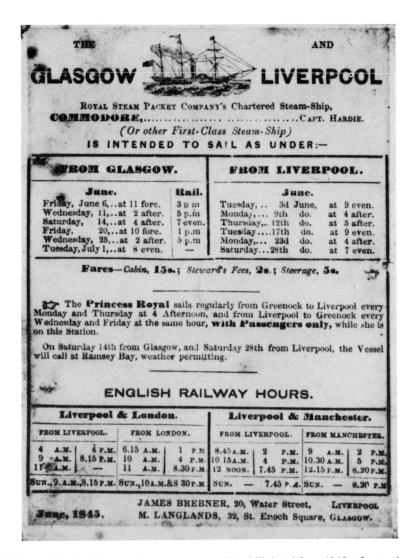

This combined railway and steam passage sailing bill dated June 1845 refers to the Royal Steam Packet Company's ship *Commodore* which maintained a service between Glasgow and Liverpool.

A Frenchman, Jacques Perier, got as far as the construction of a steam vessel in 1775 but his demonstration on the River Seine was a total failure and Perier retired defeated.

Another Frenchman met with greater success in a steam paddle-boat named *Pyroscaphe*. This attempt by the Marquis de Jouffroy d'Abbans took place on the River Saone near Lyons when the ship, powered by a James Watt engine, made progress against the current of the river for fifteen minutes on the 15th July, 1783.

Meanwhile in America, an inventor and engineer named John Fitch had been studying reports of these previous trials and in 1785 he submitted a paper to the American Philosophical Society in Philadelphia. His first steamship which took to the water during the following year, although not traditionally paddle propelled, is worthy of note. On each side of the vessel were six twelve-foot oars powered by steam, so arranged that by a complicated linkage six oars were pulling against the water, whilst the remaining oars prepared to enter in turn. John Fitch designed several other steamboats, none of which met with any great success, and it was left to another American, Richard Fulton, to achieve some commercial acclaim.

Fulton, born in Pennsylvania in 1765, was neither an inventor nor a professional engineer. He was, however, a shrewd businessman capable of learning by the mistakes of others and he fully foresaw the possibilities of steamboats. His vessel, the *Clermont*, first tried out on the Hudson River on the 17th August, 1807, was said to be a combination of the best ideas from Symington's *Charlotte Dundas* and the patents of John Fitch.

The first paddle steamer to run commercially in Europe was the *Comet* of 1812, built at Glasgow for Henry Bell. In August of that year she became the first passenger steamship carrying intrepid and often frightened men and women from Glasgow to Greenoch. Henry Bell was strongly against the practice of tipping, his advertisements stating in no uncertain terms that 'the terms are fixed for the present at four shillings for the best cabin and three shillings for the second, but beyond these rates nothing is to be allowed to servants or any other person employed about the vessel'.

Thus, it was from the efforts of these inventors, financiers and engineers that the paddle steamer was conceived, launched and operated.

BRILLIANT

The Diamond Steam Packet Company opened a service between London and Gravesend in 1836 at fares of 1/- (5p.) for the fore cabin and 1/6d. (7½p.) for the chief cabin. Among their vessels was the *Brilliant* which had been built at Poplar in 1823. The company's ships were easily recognised by a rather startling design of funnel décor. Below a black top were four lines of diamonds extending to the base. However in this illustration from an old water-colour painting the design appears to be black and white squares rather than diamonds.

The company discontinued services in 1855 following lack of patronage brought about by opposition and cheap fares from the railways and the Diamond fleet was sold the following year.

PRINCE OF WALES

Seen here at Menai is the *Prince of Wales* dating from 1846 and of 328 gross tons. In 1847 she sailed under the command of Captain W. H. Warren R.N. from Liverpool to Menai every Wednesday and Saturday at 10 a.m. returning at 9 a.m. on Mondays and Fridays. At this period it was quite common for steamers to be captained by officers of the Royal Navy who were not required on the active list.

By 1881 the *Prince of Wales* was sailing to Rhyl carrying cargo as well as passengers. After an active life of thirty-seven years she was broken up in July 1883.

CHANCELLOR

In 1856 the Stokes Bay and Isle of Wight Ferry Company was formed to provide an additional service to the Isle of Wight. In May 1863 they purchased and received the 161 gross tons steamer *Chancellor*. Besides maintaining a ferry service, her new owners ran excursions to various Island Piers.

On the *Chancellor*'s second excursion to Ventnor Pier (at that time still under construction), which took place on the 1st July, 1863, despite the fact that she was forty-five minutes behind schedule, on an ebbing tide, she was put alongside and her passengers landed. It was thought that the ship would ground whilst the passengers were ashore and the flood tide would refloat her before the time came to return. Unfortunately she was holed and began to take water and despite efforts to shore up with timber the *Chancellor* settled by her bows. During the night, helped by a freshening wind, she moved broadside to the beach and in doing so broke her back, becoming a total loss.

BLACK EAGLE NO. 1

Scene of disaster. In this early undated photograph are seen the remains of the wooden Bristol paddler *Black Eagle No. 1* probably employed as a tug on the River Avon. It would appear that the ship had suffered a boiler explosion of some magnitude, a not uncommon experience in the very early days of paddle steamships when boilers were pressurised to their maximum in attempts to produce an extra knot or two of speed, in attempts to outrival opposing companies.

SAILINGS

OF THE

Campbelton Steamers

IN

AUGUST, 1860.

The SPLENDID   STEAMERS

DRUID, - - - - Capt. Kerr.
CELT, - - - - - Capt. Finnick.

Will Sail between Glasgow, Greenock, and Campbelton, calling off Lochranza
and Carradale (weather permitting) as follows:

FROM GLASGOW.			FROM CAMPBELTON.			
	Train.					
Wednesday	1st, at half-past 10 a.m.	12 Noon.	Wednesday	1st,	at	9 A.M.
Thursday	2nd, at half-past 10 a.m.	12 Noon.	Thursday	2nd,	at	9 A.M.
Saturday	4th, at half-past 10 a.m.	12 Noon.	Saturday	4th,	at	9 A.M.
Monday *	6th,	2 P.M.	Monday *	6th,		
Tuesday	7th, at half-past 10 a.m.	12 Noon.	Tuesday	7th,	at	9 A.M.
Wednesday	8th, at half-past 10 a.m.	12 Noon.	Wednesday	8th,	at	9 A.M.
Thursday	9th, at half-past 10 a.m.	12 Noon.	Friday	10th,	at	9 A.M.
Saturday	11th, at half-past 10 a.m.	12 Noon.	Saturday	11th,	at	9 A.M.
Monday *	13th,	2 P.M.	Monday *	13th,		
Tuesday	14th, at half-past 10 a.m.	12 Noon.	Tuesday	14th,	at	9 A.M.
Wednesday	15th, at half-past 10 a.m.	12 Noon.	Wednesday	15th,	at	9 A.M.
Thursday	16th, at half-past 10 a.m.	12 Noon.	Thursday	16th,	at	9 A.M.
Saturday	18th, at half-past 10 a.m.	12 Noon.	Saturday	18th,	at	9 A.M.
Monday *	20th,	2 P.M.	Monday *	20th,		
Tuesday	21st, at half-past 10 a.m.	12 Noon.	Tuesday	21st,	at	9 A.M.
Wednesday	22nd, at half-past 10 a.m.	12 Noon.	Wednesday	22nd,	at	9 A.M.
Thursday	23rd, at half-past 10 a.m.	12 Noon.	Thursday	23rd,	at	9 A.M.
Saturday	25th, at half-past 10 a.m.	12 Noon.	Saturday	25th,	at	9 A.M.
Monday *	27th,	2 P.M.	Monday *	27th,		
Tuesday	28th, at half-past 10 a.m.	12 Noon.	Tuesday	28th,	at	9 A.M.
Wednesday	29th, at half-past 10 a.m.	12 Noon.	Wednesday	29th	at	9 A.M.
Thursday	30th, at half-past 10 a.m.	12 Noon	Thursday	30th,	at	9 A.M.

* In addition to the above Sailings, one of the Steamers will start from Campbelton every
Monday morning during the month at 6 o'Clock for Greenock, and is expected to overtake
the 11.30. Train; returning thence on the arrival of the 2 p.m. Train from Glasgow. Pass-
engers from Glasgow on Saturday, returning to Greenock on Monday, may have Return
Tickets. Fares—Cabin, 5s.; Steerage, 3s. Passengers on Monday from Campbelton to
Greenock, returning same day, to be charged the single fare only, viz. :—

FARES—CABIN, 4s.; STEERAGE, 2s.

Freight on Goods to Arran and Carradale, must be paid before going on Board.
Freight on Goods per Steamer paid on Delivery.
Goods and Cattle must be on the Quay ONE HOUR before the time of Sailing.
Passengers must look after their personal Luggage, as the Company will not be respon-
sible for any article whatever, unless *booked* and *signed* before being Shipped.

Apply to Mr. PETER STEWART, Campbelton; Messrs. D. M'LARTY
& Co., Excise Buildings, Greenock; or here, to

JOHN M'MICHAEL,

GLASGOW, July 27th, 1860.   22 Anderston Quay.

SPITTAL AND ALISON, PRINTERS, 98 UNION STREET.

SAILINGS

OF THE

Campbelton Steamers

IN

DECEMBER, 1860.

The **SPLENDID**   **STEAMERS**

DRUID, - - - -   Capt. Kerr.

CELT, - - - - -   Capt. Eaglesom.

Will Sail between Glasgow, Greenock, and Campbelton, calling off Lochranza
(unless prevented by any unforeseen circumstance) as follows:—

FROM GLASCOW

EVERY

TUESDAY, THURSDAY, AND SATURDAY,

WITH THE ADDITION OF MONDAY, THE 31st.

AT EIGHT A.M.—TRAIN, NINE A.M.

FROM CAMPBELTON

EVERY

TUESDAY, THURSDAY, AND SATURDAY,

WITH THE ADDITION OF MONDAY, THE 31st.

AT EIGHT O'CLOCK A.M.

FARES—CABIN, 4s.; STEERAGE, 2s.

N.B.—There will be no Steamer to or from Campbelton or Glasgow on
Tuesday, the 1st January, 1861.

Freight on Goods to Arran must be paid before going on Board.

Freight on Goods per Steamer paid on Delivery.

Goods and Cattle must be on the Quay ONE HOUR before the time of Sailing.

Passengers must look after their personal Luggage, as the Company will not be responsible for any article whatever, unless *booked* and *signed* before being Shipped.

Apply to Mr. PETER STEWART, Campbelton; Messrs. D. M'LARTY
& Co., Excise Buildings, Greenock; or here, to

JOHN M'MICHAEL,

GLASCOW, *Nov. 28th,* 1860.   22 Anderston Quay.

SPITTAL AND ALISON, PRINTERS, 98 UNION STREET.

By 1860, the date of this sailing bill, regular services were provided by 'The Splendid
Steamers' *Druid* and *Celt* between Glasgow and Campbeltown.

It was a regular practice in those days to print the names of the ship Masters and
regular passengers would often put themselves to considerable trouble to travel with
the Captain of their choice.

Although racing was officially discouraged the smoke and steam emitting from these three Scottish steamers bears witness to some form of rivalry. They are, nearest the camera, the *Marquis of Bute* (1868), *Neptune* (1892) and *Chancellor* (1880).

"*Vivid*"

VIVID

By the time the *Vivid* had been constructed by Barclay Curle and Company in 1864 some consideration was being made for the comfort of passengers by the construction of a small deck saloon aft of the funnel for first class passengers.

When broken up in 1902, the *Vivid* had the distinction of possessing the last steeple engine in service on the Clyde. She is seen here at speed wearing the colours of the North British Railway with whose fleet she served from 1887.

VELINDRA

The Pockett family of Swansea did much to popularise excursions in the Bristol Channel. James Wathen Pockett purchased the *Velindra* of 1860 some seven years later when her owners the Cardiff Steam Navigation Company went into liquidation. An iron paddler of 199 gross tons with a fair turn of speed, she was placed under the command of Captain William Pockett. The *Swansea Herald* commented favourably

on a crossing in 3 hours 58 minutes from Swansea to Bristol on 23rd July, 1868.

When her owner died in 1890 she ran for seven more years under the ownership of Pockett's Bristol Channel Steam Packet Company, then the ageing vessel was sold to John Hurley of Bristol who broke her up at Clevedon, Avon.

The *Velindra* is seen here turning by Ilfracombe Pier.

Mid-day on a summer morning and the only signs of life are the steam-train at the Pier Head and three strollers making their way along the planking whilst two others lean over the railings watching the water.

The steamers moored to the Royal Pier at Southampton are the *Carisbrooke* (1876), *Prince Leopold* (1876) and on the extreme right, *Her Majesty* (1885).

STEAMER

"SCOTIA"

Captain Buchanan.

WEDNESDAY, 26th MAY, 1880.

Menu.

LUNCHEON.

Cold Roast.   Cold Corned Beef,   Hot Potatoes.
Sardines.   Biscuits and Cheese.

DINNER.

Fish.
Salmon.

Joints.
Roast Beef.   Corned Beef.   Roast Lamb.
Chicken and Ham.

Sweets.
Custard and Apple Tart.

Cheese.   Salad.

Dessert.

This ornate menu dated 26th May, 1880, gives the details of the meals available on board the paddle steamer *Scotia*, under the command of Captain Buchanan in her first year of service for Buchanan Steamers Ltd., whilst on the Glasgow to Rothesay sailings.

BICKERSTAFFE

Sailing past the world-famous Blackpool Tower and pleasure park is the *Bickerstaffe* built in 1879 by Lairds of Birkenhead, for service from Blackpool. Of 197 gross tons she was finally broken up at Garston in 1928.

The Pier at Ilfracombe in 1888 shows four widely differing Bristol Channel excursion steamers tied sponson to sponson. The photograph was probably taken on a Bank Holiday weekend after the vessels had disembarked their passengers for a few hours on shore.

The paddle steamers are, left to right: *Lady Margaret* (1883), the twin-funnelled *Velindra* (1860), *Waverley* (1885) and *Bonnie Doon* (1876).

The hey-day of the paddler is exemplified by this photograph taken in 1882 of the North Pier at Blackpool showing three excursion steamers with their decks packed with passengers. The vessels are, left to right, the *Great Britain*, also used as a tug, the *Roses* belonging to the Morecambe Steamboat Company, and the aptly named, *Queen of the Bay*, owned by the Blackpool Pier Company.

These newspaper advertisements from the *Bournemouth Observer* of September 1886
show the sailings operated by the Bournemouth, Swanage and Poole Steam Packet
Company, a local company and the Bournemouth, Swanage, Weymouth and Torquay Steam Packet Company. The latter was the title given at Bournemouth to the
vessels of Cosens and Company, Weymouth, in an attempt to capture local custom.

At this time both companies were operating in direct competition. The reference
to 'The Splendid Saloon Steamer' *Princess Helena* by the local concern is interesting
in that during September 1886 she had been chartered from her Southampton owners
as a temporary replacement for the paddle steamer *Bournemouth*, which had foundered during the previous month.

WINDSOR CASTLE

In 1891 the Bournemouth, Swanage and Poole Steam Packet Company ordered from the Southampton Naval Works, the *Windsor Castle*, the largest excursion steamer yet to be seen on the South Coast. Entering service during the following year her owners' expectations were not fulfilled, for she proved to be too large for the number of passengers available, and had an extensive appetite for coal. In 1895 she was purchased by a Scottish concern, the Glasgow, Ayrshire and Campbeltown Steamboat Company and sailed from Princes Pier to Campbeltown via Dunoon, Fairlie, Keppel, Lochranza, Pirnmill and Machrie. She was renamed *Culzean Castle*. Despite an extensive overhaul she suffered several breakdowns and after two seasons was sold to Clyde Excursion Steamers Ltd. for cruises from the Broomielaw, Glasgow, under the name of *Carrick Castle*.

By 1900 her third owners had had enough of this unfortunate vessel and being unable to find a local buyer she was sold to the Russian-owned Chinese Eastern Railway. Renamed yet again as the *Nagadan*, she sailed from Port Arthur and when the Russo-Japanese War broke out in 1904 saw service as a fleet auxiliary. During the advance of the Japanese she was captured intact and sailed under their flag as the *Nagara Maru* and later as the *Tenri Naru*.

In November 1931 the old *Windsor Castle* went aground at Matsu Shima, Japan, whilst running an inter-island service and became a total loss, thus ending the career of a vessel which had a chequered career under many owners, flags and names.

With umbrellas acting as sunshades the *Windsor Castle* leaves Bournemouth Pier, her siren sounding the signal for going astern.

JUPITER

With her Captain ready to telegraph his orders and members of the crew at readiness on the sponson, the Clyde paddler *Jupiter* gives an impression of speed and power as she cuts through the water in the 1890's.

This example of a weekly handbill for excursions from the south coast resort of Bournemouth during July 1899 shows the extraordinary variety of trips that the would-be passenger could choose from. These were maintained by two vessels with assistance only from Cosen and Company's steamer *Empress* on the Bournemouth to Swanage service.

The longest trip was of about 5¼ hours to Torquay and return with an option of returning from Torquay by train should the condition of the sea prove unsuitable for the passenger.

An appealing trip to honeymooners and courting couples was the 'Pleasant Moonlight Excursion' of 1½ hours duration. It can only be hoped that Bournemouth and South Coast Steam Packets Limited had some arrangement with the clerk of the weather to ensure in fact that moonlight was available on these occasions!

Bank Holiday Monday at Ilfracombe Pier. The date is 1894 and the steamers, left to right, are *Lorna Doone* (1891), *Westward Ho* (1894), *Brodick Castle* (1878), *Earl of Dunraven* (1888), *Brighton* (1878) and *Ravenswood* (1891). All were regular Bristol Channel vessels with the exception of *Brodick Castle* which was on charter to a Bristol Syndicate for that season only.

The three small boys perched on the railing seem more interested in the camera than the magnificent array of steamships.

The Favourite Steamers
"BRODICK CASTLE"
"LORD ELGIN"

Daily

Excursions.

July 22nd
TO
July 29th,
1899.

Bournemouth & Swanage Daily Service. Return Fare 2/- 1st class, 1/6 2nd
Increased Accommodation. The LORD ELGIN in conjunction with the EMPRESS will leave
BOURNEMOUTH FOR SWANAGE at 10.30, 11, 12.30, 2.30, 3, 4.30, 5.15 and 6.15.
SWANAGE FOR BOURNEMOUTH at 8.45, 9.30, 11.30, 12.15, 1.15, 3.30, 4.30 and 5.30.
BOSCOMBE FOR BOURNEMOUTH & SWANAGE at 10. 10.30, and 2.30.
Steamer leaving Swanage at 8.45, 9.30, 12.15, 1.15, 4.30 & 5.30 proceeds to Bournemouth & Boscombe.
On WEDNESDAY AFTERNOONS a later boat will leave Swanage at 7 o'clock, returning from Bourne-
mouth at 7.45. On Thursday the 4.30 Swanage Boat will not go to Boscombe

Saturday, July 22nd.
COWES and PORTSMOUTH (Calling at Yarmouth).
Leaving Swanage 9.30, Bournemouth 10.30, Boscombe 10.40, Yarmouth 11.45. Returning from
Portsmouth at 3.30, Cowes 4 30, Yarmouth at 5.15.
Return Fares - From Bournemouth or Boscombe to Cowes, 3/- 1st, 2/6 2nd ; Portsmouth, 4/- 1st,
3 - 2nd ; Yarmouth, 2/6 1st, 2 - 2nd. From Swanage or Poole 6d. extra. Tourist Tickets avail-
able for return by either "Monarch' or " Brodick Castle " during Season 1/- extra.
Leave Poole 9.0, Sandbanks 9.20 for Bournemouth. Returning at 6.30. Single Fare 6d.

Monday, July 24th.
**A Cruise up the interesting HARBOUR of PORTSMOUTH, to view the Dock-
yards, Ironclads, Porchester Castle, &c. and passing the Racing Yachts in
Cowes Roads.**
RYDE & PORTSMOUTH (Calling at Yarmouth).
Leaving Swanage 9.30, Bournemouth 10.30, Boscombe 10.40, Yarmouth 11.45.
Returning from Portsmouth at 3.45, Ryde at 4.0, Yarmouth at 5.0.
Return Fares from Bournemouth or Boscombe to Ryde or Portsmouth, 4/- 1st class, 3/- 2nd class.
Yarmouth 2/6 " 2/- "
From Swanage or Poole 6d. extra. Tourist Tickets available for retur by either " Monarch " or
" Brodick Castle " during Season 1/- extra.
Leave Poole 9, Sandbanks 9.20 for Bournemouth. Returning at 6.30 p.m. Single Fare 6d.

PLEASANT MOONLIGHT EXCURSION
Leaving Bournemouth at 8.15. Returning thereto at 9.45. Fare 1/- Season Ticket Holders 6d.

Tuesday, July 25th.
TORQUAY. Two Hours at Torquay.
Leaving Boscombe 8.20 snarp (by " Lord Elgin "), Bournemouth 8.40, Swanage 9.15, returning
from Torquay at 4 o'clock to Swanage, Bournemouth and Boscombe, arriving home about 9.15.
Fare 5 6 1st class, 4 6 2nd.
Season Ticket Holders of both Bournemouth Companies Half First-class Fare.
Passengers desiring to return by rail may do so at Reduced Rates by train leaving Torquay at 2.57,
due Bournemouth 7.15, Swanage 8.52 ; or leaving Torquay 4.18, due Bournemouth (only) 10.17,
by production of Coupon to be obtained on the steamer.

Wednesday, July 26th.
SOUTHAMPTON (Direct).
Leaving Boscombe at 10.0, Bournemouth at 10.30. Returning from Southampton at 2.0 o'clock.
RETURN FARE 2/- ONLY.

Evening Excursion Round the Great Breakwater and Training Ships in
PORTLAND ROADS About 60 Miles for 1/6.
Leaving Boscombe at 4.0, Bournemouth at 4.30, arriving home at 9 p.m.
Leave Poole at 9.0, Sandbanks 9.20, Swanage for Bournemouth 9.30. Returning at 9.15 p.m.
Single Fare 6d.

SWANAGE
Leaving Bournemouth at 2.30, 3, 4.30, and 5.15 (Boscombe
at 2 30 and 5.30). Returning at 3.30, 4.30, 5.30 and 7 o'clock.
Fare ONE SHILLING.

Thursday, July 27th.
TOTLAND (Isle of Wight) COWES & PORTSMOUTH
Leaving Swanage 9.30, Bournemouth 10.30, Boscombe 10.40, Totland Bay 11.45. Giving 5
hours at Totland and 3 Cowes. Returning from Portsmouth at 3.15, Cowes at 4, Totland Bay
at 5 p.m.

			1st class	2nd class
Return Fares from Bournemouth or Boscombe to	Cowes		3/-	2/6
"	"	Portsmouth	4/-	3 -
"	"	Totland	2/-	1 6

From Swanage or Poole 6d. extra. Tourist Tickets available for return by either " Monarch "
or " Brodick Castle " during Season 1/- extra.
Leave Poole 9.0, Sandbanks 9.20, for Bournemouth. Returning at 6.15 p.m. Single fare, 6d.

Friday, July 28th.
Round the ISLE OF WIGHT, VENTNOR and RYDE
Calling at and giving Two Hours at Ventnor or Ryde.
Leaving Swanage 9.30, Bournemouth 10.30, Boscombe 10.40. Returning from Ryde at 4,
on arrival of the train leaving Ventnor at 3.12.
See Railway and Tourist Arrangements below.
Return Fares from Bournemouth or Boscombe, 4/6 1st, 3/6 2nd. Single to Ventnor or Ryde,
3/- 1st, 2/6 2nd
From Swanage or Poole, 6d. extra. Leave Poole at 9.0, Sandbanks 9.20, for Bournemouth.
Returning at 6.15 p.m. Single Fare 6d.

Saturday, July 29th.
Morning Cruise Round the Magnificent HARBOUR of POOLE
Leaving Boscombe at 10, Bournemouth 10.20, and returning thereto at 1 p.m. Fare 1 6.

Afternoon Excursion to WEYMOUTH Direct, for 2/-
Two Hours at Weymouth.
Leaving Boscombe at 2.30, Bournemouth at 3. Returning from Weymouth at 7.
Single to Poole at 9.15 p.m., 6d.

SEASON TICKETS :
SEASON TICKETS to run from March 27th to end of season in October, may now be obtained
on the following terms :—
FIRST TICKET, £2 2s. 0d. ; SECOND TICKET in same family, £1 1s. 0d. ; Third and subsequent
Tickets in same family, 15/- each. Children under Twelve Years, 10/6 each. Resident
Clerks or Shop Assistants, 15/- each.

**FIRST-CLASS REFRESHMENTS of all kinds, Hot and Cold Luncheons and Teas,
at Moderate Charges, in the Dining Saloon.**

RAILWAY ARRANGEMENTS.
On production of their Steamer Ticket at Ventnor or Shanklin Stations passengers travel by rail
from thence to Ryde Pier Head to rejoin the Steamer at Special Fares. First Class, 2/3 ;
Second Class, 1/6 ; or from Sandown, First Class, 1.9 ; Second Class, 1 3.

Bicycles 6d. each single journey. Dogs charged Full Passenger Fare. Deck Chairs 1d. each.

AGENTS FOR SEASON TICKETS, &c.
Mr. A. J. Abbott, No. 2, Boscombe Chambers, Boscombe ; Mr. E. J. Thompson, The Post Office,
Westbourne ; Mr. A. J. Ward, Steam Packet Office, Swanage ; Mr. C. J. Hearson, Quay Street,
Yarmouth ; Mr. John Mowlam, Poole ; Mr. H. E. Scanlan, Office of s.s. " Telegraph," The
Quay, Poole

The Directors reserve to themselves the right to alter the above Programme, as the weather or
other circumstances may require.
BY ORDER, **EDWARD BICKER, Secretary.**
BOURNEMOUTH AND SOUTH COAST STEAM PACKETS, LIMITED.
Offices : *Wilts and Dorset Bank Chambers, Bournemouth.*

W Mate & Sons Ltd. *Directory Office, Bournemouth.*

The *Viceroy* (1875), *Sultan* (1862) and *Sultana* (1868) were posed against a typical Scottish background when this photograph was taken near the turn of the century.

No sign of impropriety as these Edwardian passengers disembark from the paddler *Bilsdale* on a trip from Yarmouth to Lowestoft before the First World War.

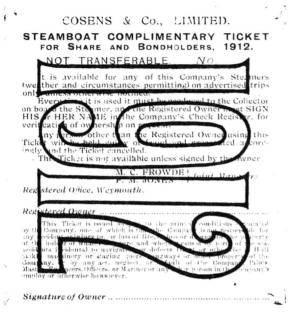

COSENS & Co., LIMITED.

STEAMBOAT COMPLIMENTARY TICKET
FOR SHARE AND BONDHOLDERS, 1912.

NOT TRANSFERABLE.   No

t is available for any of this Company's Steamers
(weather and circumstances permitting) on advertised trips
only unless otherwise notified.

Every time it is used it must be produced to the Collector
on board the Steamer, and the Registered Owner must SIGN
HIS or HER NAME in the Company's Check Register, for
verification of ownership on production.

Any person other than the Registered Owner using this
Ticket will be held guilty of fraud and prosecuted accordingly, and the Ticket cancelled.

This Ticket is not available unless signed by the owner

M. C. FROWDE, Joint Managers
F. M. JONES,

Registered Office, Weymouth.

Registered Owner ....

This Ticket is issued subject to the printed conditions circulated
by the Company, one of which is that the Company is not responsible for
any accident or injury to, or loss of life, or loss or damage to the property
of the holder of whatever nature and whether caused by perils of the sea,
accidents incidental to navigation, or defects latent or otherwise. Hull
tackle, machinery or staging, piers, gangways or other property of the
Company, or by any act, neglect or default of the Company, Pilots,
Master Engineers, Officers, or Mariner or any other person in the Company's
employ or otherwise howsoever.

Signature of Owner ....

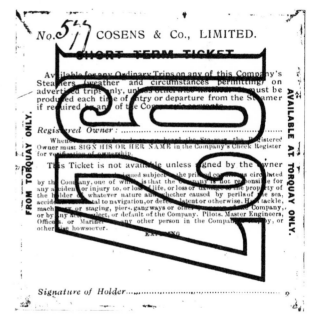

No. 5   COSENS & Co., LIMITED.

SHORT TERM TICKET

Available for any Ordinary Trips on any of this Company's
Steamers (weather and circumstances permitting) on
advertised trips only, unless otherwise notified, must be
produced each time of entry or departure from the Steamer
if required by any of the Company's servants.

Registered Owner : ....

Whenever joining or leaving the Steamer, the Registered
Owner must SIGN HIS OR HER NAME in the Company's Check Register
for verification of ownership.

This Ticket is not available unless signed by the owner

Issued subject to the printed conditions circulated
by the Company, one of which is that the Company is not responsible for
any accident or injury to, or loss of life, or loss or damage to the property of
the holder of whatever nature and whether caused by perils of the sea,
accidents incidental to navigation, or defect latent or otherwise. Hull tackle,
machinery or staging, piers, gangways or other property of the Company,
or by any act, neglect, or default of the Company, Pilots, Master Engineers,
Officers, or Mariner or any other person in the Company's employ, or
otherwise howsoever.

EXPIRING

AVAILABLE AT TORQUAY ONLY.

FROM TORQUAY ONLY.

Signature of Holder ....

Steamer operators realised the benefit to be accrued from issuing short- and long-term season tickets and by the late 19th century these were advertised on sailing bills and newspaper advertisements. Those issued by the Bournemouth, Boscombe, Swanage and Weymouth Steam Packet Company, more commonly known as Cosens and Company of Weymouth, were pocket-sized cardboard and fabric-covered tickets with the Company's name printed boldly on the outside and space for the signature of the owner on the obverse. These tickets were generally available for any excursion throughout the life of the ticket except for special long-distance trips such as those operated across the Channel to Cherbourg and the Channel Islands. For excursions such as these the season ticket holder expected to pay but at a much reduced fare, an example being a voyage advertised to take place on Thursday, 19th July, 1888, from Bournemouth to Cherbourg at a normal fare of 10/6d. (52½p.), season ticket holders being invited to sail at half fare.

Often subsequent members of the family could obtain season tickets at a reduced price as could servants and sometimes shop assistants.

After the 1914–18 war, the popularity of season tickets declined, but fifty years later P. & A. Campbell Ltd. was encouraging would-be passengers to purchase vouchers at the commencement of the season at a much reduced rate, for the paddle excursions of their choice.

2 Transatlantic Crossings

Once the steam engine had become established as generally reliable, its use in ships destined to traverse the oceans of the world became an established fact. The advantages of having a form of propulsion which neither relied on wind nor tide were apparent. For the first time owners could give an accurate departure time in all but the very worst weather conditions and a reasonable estimation of when the paddle steamer would arrive at its destination thousands of miles away. Despite these obvious advantages there were factors on the debit side as well. The amount of space needed for engines, boilers and coal took up room that could have carried profitable cargo. Whilst coal was plentiful and cheap in Britain, should the vessel have to be re-bunkered at foreign ports, fuel would often have to be transported there from distant mines, thus adding to expense. The travelling public were keen on record crossings but speed could only be attained at a cost of increased fuel consumption. Thus, although the advent of steam caused an upsurge in the awareness and use of shipping, all these factors had to be carefully balanced in estimating cargo and passenger tariffs.

It was to the Atlantic that ship-owners turned their eyes, realising the great potential that a regular service between America and Britain would bring. The first eastward crossing was made in 1819 by the American-owned *Savannah*, originally constructed as a schooner but fitted with an auxiliary steam engine and collapsible paddle wheels, which gave her a speed of some four knots. Under the command of Captain Moses Rogers she left for Liverpool on the 19th May, 1819, but although credited as being the first paddle steamer to cross the Atlantic, it appears that her engines were only used for a very small proportion of the crossing which took twenty-seven days and eleven hours.

The *Savannah* made the return crossing entirely under sail and it was not until two years later that the westward journey was attempted by steamship. This voyage was undertaken by an oddity, the *Rising Star*, built on the Thames in 1821 with three keels and paddle wheels set either side of the centre keel. Built as a warship for Chile, she left Gravesend for Valparaiso on the 22nd October,

1821, and eventually arrived, after repairs in Ireland, on the 22nd April, 1822. Once again the greater part of the voyage was made under sail, her seventy nautical horse power engines being used only as an auxiliary means of progress.

Not for another fifteen years was the mighty Atlantic to be conquered entirely by steam and paddle, the occasion being the well-known 'race' between the diminutive paddler *Sirius* of the St. George Steam Packet Company and Brunel's *Great Western*. It was the event which led to the possibility of regular transatlantic services and mail contracts.

The first regular transatlantic service for mail and passengers came into being by the efforts of Samuel Cunard, a merchant and shipowner of Halifax, Nova Scotia. When Cunard signed a contract between himself and the British Lords of the Admiralty on the 4th May, 1839, the proposed service was for seven years from Liverpool and the stipulation was made that a naval officer had to be carried on each voyage. The sailings were to be twice monthly and the remuneration fixed at £55,000 per year.

Cunard discussed arrangements with Robert Napier for three vessels of about eight hundred tons to be constructed at a cost of £30,000 each. Napier, however, felt that the proposed vessels were not adequate for a regular transatlantic service throughout the year and he offered to put Cunard in touch with other merchants with a view to raising the extra capital needed for larger and more powerful vessels. The outcome was the formation of 'The Glasgow Propriety in the British and North American Steam Packets', the direct ancestor of the Cunard Company of today. Napier and Cunard were able to go ahead with the construction of four vessels, each of one thousand two hundred tons, and with four hundred and twenty nautical horse power engines. The British Admiralty agreed to the changes and increased the annual remuneration to £60,000.

No time was lost in the construction of the vessels and on the 5th February, 1840, the *Britannia* was launched, but despite day and night working there was little prospect of the ship being ready for the original sailing date of the 4th June set by Cunard. The British Government agreed that the start could be delayed and that the commencement of regular services need not occur until the autumn.

Exactly one month later, on the 4th July, 1840, *Britannia* embarked sixty-three passengers and, under the command of Captain Henry Woodruff R.N., set sail at 2.00 p.m. from the River Mersey to Halifax, N.S., and Boston. Thirteen days later she arrived to a salute from the frigate *Winchester* at Halifax. After a stay of only eight hours she immediately set sail for Boston where she arrived at 10.00 p.m. on Saturday, 19th July, her voyage from Liverpool having taken fourteen days, eight hours.

Thus it was that Cunard's steamships commenced their transatlantic services, to be operated mainly by paddle steamers for the next forty-five years.

THE TRANSATLANTIC PIONEERS

The original four ships built for The Glasgow Propriety in the British and North American Steam Packets were sub-contracted.

Name	Constructor	Maiden Voyage	Commander
Britannia	R. Duncan	4 July 1840	Capt. H. Woodruff
Acadia	John Wood	4 August 1840	Capt. E. C. Miller
Caledonia	R. Wood	4 September 1840	Capt. R. Cleland
Columbia	R. Steele	4 October 1840	Capt. Ewing

All were: Length 207 ft. Beam 34 ft. 4 in. Depth 24 ft. 4 in.

TRANSATLANTIC TIMINGS

Such was the quest for speed in transatlantic crossings that the Cunard paddle steamers *Britannia* and *Acadia* cut down their crossing times by well over two days within just over two years. Recorded times are:

Date	Ship	Crossing	Days/Hours	Average Speed
July 1840	*Britannia*	Westward	12/10	8.50 knots
Aug. 1840	*Acadia*	Westward	11/4	9.45 knots
July 1841	*Acadia*	Westward	10/22	9.67 knots
Aug. 1840	*Britannia*	Eastward	10/0	10.56 knots
Sept. 1842	*Acadia*	Eastward	9/15	10.97 knots

The distance involved was 2,534 nautical miles.

By the 1850's the American Government, realising that Samuel Cunard had obtained a strong hold on the transatlantic traffic, entered into an agreement with a Mr. Collins to form the Collins Line, with the avowed intent of capturing their own share of the ever-increasing trade. At first the new line more than held its own against the Cunard paddlers and the Collins Line ships, *Atlantic*, *Arctic*, *Pacific* and *Baltic*, surpassed the Cunarders in size and elegance. In the year 1852 they carried four thousand three hundred passengers whilst the Cunard total was under three thousand.

Unfortunately, the American company was to meet with severe misfortune when one of the quartet, the *P.S. Arctic*, was run down and sunk by a French vessel on the 27th September, 1854, with heavy loss of life. Two years later another of the Collins Line vessels, the *P.S. Pacific*, returning from Liverpool to New York, was lost without trace. The company never fully recovered from this dual blow and failed in February, 1858, their remaining ships being laid up in New York.

SIRIUS

The *Sirius* of 1837 was built by Robert Menzies and Son in Scotland and powered by a 320 N.H.P. side-lever engine constructed by Thomas Wingate and Company whose works were at Whiteinch near Glasgow.

Owned by the British and American Steam Navigation Company she became the first vessel to cross the Atlantic under continuous steam power. Leaving Cork on the 4th April, 1838, she arrived at New York on the 22nd, after 18 days and 10 hours of continuous steaming, at an average speed of 6.7 knots.

By the middle of the 19th century, paddle-operated steamships dominated the Atlantic trade and continued to do so until gradually replaced by faster and more economic screw steamers during the latter quarter of the century. By 1900, paddle propulsion had been entirely superseded but before leaving the Atlantic mention must be made of the only paddle prop. transatlantic crossing of the 20th century by the British-built tug *Eppleton Hall*, which sailed entirely under her own power to San Francisco during the winter of 1969–70. Built as a tug in 1914, and under the command of her owner, an American, Mr. Scott Newhall, her eleven thousand-mile journey from Newcastle with a crew of nine men and three women must rank as one of the great achievements of latter-day paddle power. She is now happily preserved and still occasionally steams under her own power across the more placid waters of San Francisco Bay.

GREAT WESTERN

Although the *Sirius* was the first vessel to cross the Atlantic entirely under her own steam, she did so by the barest of margins. The *Great Western* arrived the day after the smaller steamer that she had tried hard to overtake.

Designed by Isambard Kingdom Brunel, and constructed in 1837 at Bristol, she was 236 ft. in length. The *Great Western*'s voyage was completed at an average speed some 2 knots faster than the *Sirius*, in 15 days and 5 hours, thus becoming the first steam transatlantic record breaker.

GREAT EASTERN

The largest merchant ship in the world when constructed and the first and only five-funnelled paddle steamer are two of the claims held by Brunel's *Great Eastern*.

BRITANNIA

The *Britannia* was built following the mail contract signed between Samuel Cunard and the British Government, being one of four similar vessels proposed for the transatlantic service. Launched on the 5th February, 1840, by Miss Isabella Napier, her length was 230 ft. and the combined power of her two independent engines totalled 440 H.P.

Her voyage from Liverpool to Halifax, Nova Scotia, and Boston, Mass., which commenced on the 4th July, 1840, inaugurated the first regular mail service by steamship between Britain and the North American continent.

CONNAUGHT

The launch of the Ocean Mail Co.'s steamship *Connaught* at Jarrow on the Tyne. She was 378 ft. in length with a beam of 40 ft. and could carry 800 passengers, 200 of them in first class accommodation.

GREAT EASTERN
The *Great Eastern* engraved from a drawing by Edwin Weedon. A dramatic view
of the great ship.

The construction of the *Great Eastern* in progress at Millwall in 1857.

GREAT EASTERN

The ship, which is generally acknowledged as the most famous paddle steamer of all time, was not really a paddler in the full sense of the term, since Isambard Kingdom Brunel designed the ship to take advantage of screw propulsion and wind, as well as paddle wheels.

Much has been made of her size, which amounted to 18,915 gross tons. She was in fact the largest ship ever constructed at the time of her launch in 1858, a record which was to remain unsurpassed for nearly half a century. Brunel designed the *Great Eastern* for voyages to the Far East where little bunkering facilities existed and consequently her size was affected by the huge bunkering space needed in her hull for such an immense voyage.

Bad luck seems to have attended the vessel throughout her life, workmen being killed and maimed during her construction. It is said that Brunel who had suffered a stroke just before her sea trials, had a relapse when told about an explosion on the 9th September, 1859, caused by a blocked safety valve which caused the death of six seamen, the great engineer dying some six days later.

Due to lack of capital it was decided to place the *Great Eastern* on the transatlantic run but her ill-fortune again attended and in order to achieve some remuneration she was chartered to the Atlantic Telegraph Company. As a cable layer she met with some success, her immense hull being large enough to carry 2,000 miles of rolled cable. At her second transatlantic cable attempt the wire was successfully laid and on the 27th July, 1866, the telegraph station at Valentia in Ireland received a message from a similar station at Heart's Content, Newfoundland. Reconverted in 1867, the *Great Eastern* carried passengers visiting the World Trade Fair in France but was withdrawn afterwards until recommissioned once more as a cable layer. In 1874 she became redundant and for twelve years was laid up at Milford Haven.

Her final tour of duty came when the massive ship was purchased as a floating advertisement for a Liverpool store. In 1888 she was sold to the breakers for £16,000 and took two years to dismantle.

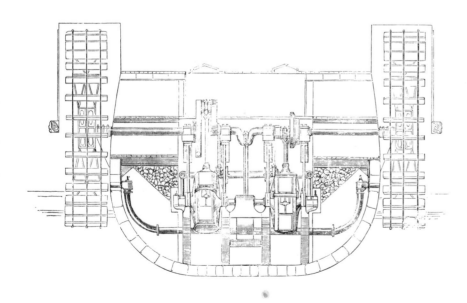

Detailed sections of the *Great Eastern*.

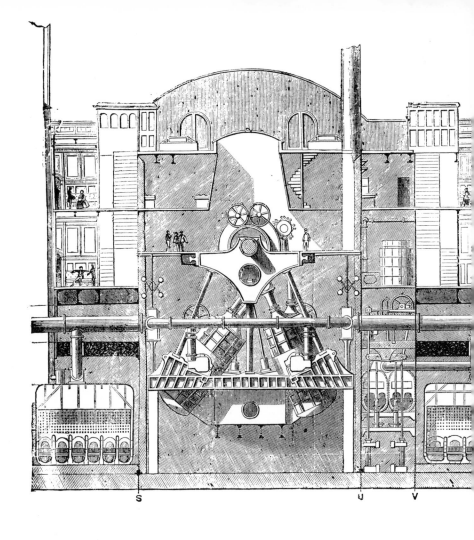

Detailed sections of the *Great Eastern*.

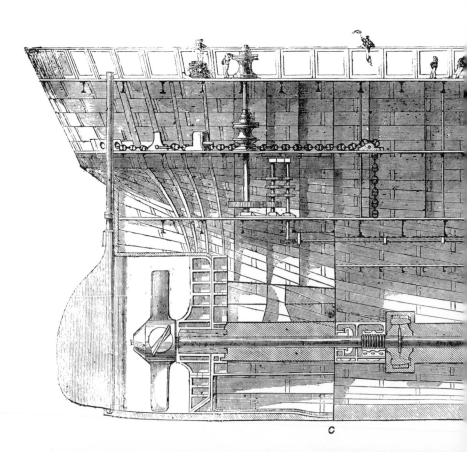

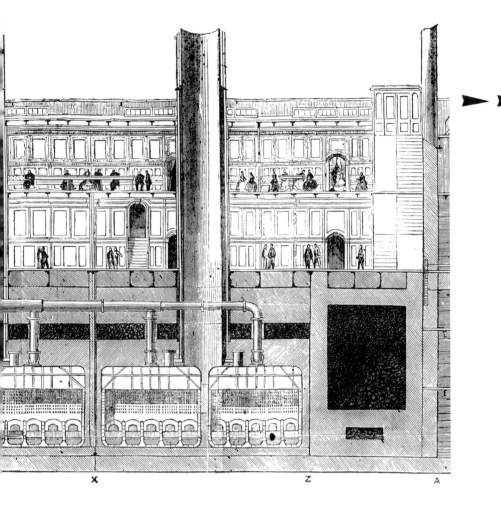

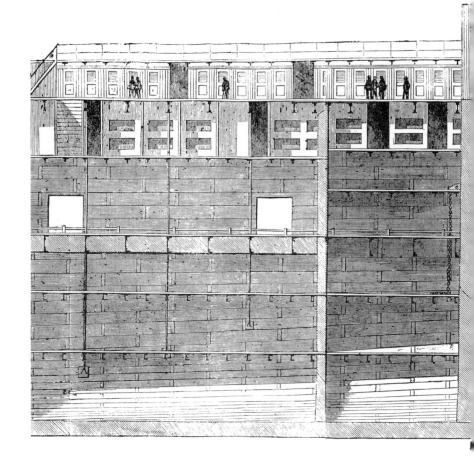

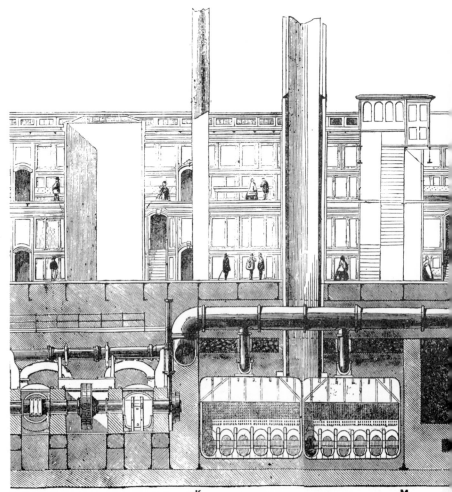

K M

G

N   P   Q

EPPLETON HALL

What will probably be the last transatlantic crossing by a paddle-propelled vessel took place during the winter of 1969–70 by the diminutive 160-ton paddle tug *Eppleton Hall*. Launched in 1914, previously engaged in towing duties in Seaham Harbour, this oil-fired paddler sailed under her own steam to Dunston-on-Tyne for scrapping on the 13th November, 1967. Various attempts were made to preserve the vessel which culminated in her purchase by Scott Newhall, an American. He sailed her to San Francisco to form part of the Maritime Museum at that port.

The voyage was not without incident; sailing on the 18th September, 1969, she voyaged through the English Channel and into the Bay of Biscay where she ran out of fuel. She had to be refuelled at sea, eventually arriving at Lisbon on the 10th October where her owner wisely fitted extra tanks.

Calling at Madeira, Las Palmas and St. Vincent, the *Eppleton Hall* arrived at Georgetown, Guyana, on the 13th December, 1969, thus making the first trans-atlantic crossing by a paddle vessel this century. The crossing from St. Vincent to Georgetown comprised a distance of 2,200 miles and like the early transatlantic steamers, the *Eppleton Hall* resorted on favourable occasions to the use of sails in order to conserve her fuel.

Having crossed the Atlantic her voyage was not yet over. After minor repairs at Port of Spain, Trinidad, the paddle tug sailed under her own steam once again through the Panama Canal and in stages along the Pacific Coast to San Francisco where she finally arrived on the 24th March, 1970. Ten days before her arrival she undertook the final task for which she was designed, when, off San Diego, she took in tow a disabled fishing boat and handed her over to the care of a coastguard cutter.

The photograph shows the *Eppleton Hall* as she sails out to sea for the first time during her trials in 1914 with her Board of Directors standing proudly on board.

The diminutive *Eppleton Hall* leaves North Shields whilst still in operational service as a tug on the 12th June, 1954.

3 Cross-Channel Traffic

Just as the increased reliability of the steam engine had brought about regular transatlantic services, the paddle-propelled steamship was soon adapted for cross-channel services to the Continent and Ireland.

The first crossing of the English Channel appears to have been made on the 17th March, 1816, when the *P.S. Margery*, which had previously worked on the Clyde and the Thames, was sold to a Paris company and sailed from Newhaven to Le Havre. During the following year, the *Caledonia*, owned by James Watt Jr., crossed from Margate to Rotterdam and thence some way up the Rhine. She eventually became the first Dutch steamboat.

It fell to a Napier-engined paddle steamer, the *Rob Roy*, to open the first regular cross-channel service in 1821, when she maintained a service from Dover to Calais. The *Rob Roy* was later purchased by the French Government to carry mail, operating under the name of *Henri Quatre* and latterly as the *Duc d'Orleans*.

By 1816 paddlers were sailing to the Isle of Man and to Ireland. The steamer *Greenock* operated daily between Belfast, Carrickfergus and Bangor and the steamers *Waterloo* and *Belfast* alternated sailings between Liverpool and Dublin.

The General Steam Navigation Company was formed by a group of London merchants in October, 1824, and operated paddle steamers along the coasts of Britain and across the Channel between Le Havre and Brest, later extending their services as far as the Mediterranean. Subsequently this company became well known for a number of excursion paddle steamers which they operated on the Thames.

From an early date the steamers were operated on a class basis, first- and second-class passengers being separated, the former being provided with adequate saloon accommodation and cabins situated towards the stern of the vessel. Second-class passengers were generally contained in the bow section which was always more vulnerable to the elements, their sleeping accommodation being hard wooden bunks. Due to competition fares remained reasonable, especially on runs which were in direct opposition to the railways and established stagecoach systems. An inconvenience to well-to-do passengers was the fact that servants were expected to travel second class, thus depriving the 'Master' of their immediate attention.

Paddle steamers of the G.S.N. Company and other coastal shipping concerns were adapted to carry freight, farm produce and even livestock, a number of regular services being operated around the coasts of Britain and Europe.

On the Continent, river traffic on the Rhine, Danube, Elbe and other waterways quickly took advantage of paddle propulsion, whilst in America coastwise steamers rapidly assisted in promoting trade and development.

The short sea passage between Britain and Europe for passengers and mail was seen by the railways as a means of connecting long-distance travel at minimum disadvantage to their passengers. Once the South Eastern Railway Company had opened lines to Folkestone in 1843 and to Dover during the following year, a succession of paddle steamers ploughed their snowy wake across the Channel. Prohibited by law to own steamers in their own right, the Railway Companies neatly dodged the issue by forming subsidiary companies to own their ships, but later obtained the necessary Parliamentary sanction to operate in their own right. The carriage of mail

'THE ALLIANCE' SOUTHAMPTON AND HAVRE MAIL STEAMER

ALLIANCE

In March 1855 the New South Western Steam Packet Company of Southampton purchased, from Ditchburn and Mare, the *Alliance* of 507 gross tons at a cost of £19,460. With accommodation for 167 passengers and a speed of 13½ knots, she was placed on service between Southampton and Le Havre under the command of Captain Walter Smith and made her maiden voyage on the 11th July, 1855.

Her schedule across the Channel was timed for a nine-hour crossing, some three hours shorter than other steam packets sailing from Southampton at that time. When withdrawn from service in 1900 she was sold to Holland and shortly afterwards broken up.

ARIADNE

One of the earliest steamships to provide a regular service between the Channel Islands and the port of Southampton was the *Ariadne*, a vessel of 195 tons and 74 N.H.P. engines. Her arrival was often not without incident as the following notice from the Guernsey *Mercury* of Saturday, 27th March, 1830, shows:

TAKE NOTICE

In consequence of the great confusion arising every time the *Ariadne* arrives at Guernsey, occasioned by the number of boats that come alongside at the same moment, and the watermen jumping on board the vessel and taking hold and putting into their boats the passengers' luggage, against every effort of the Captain, a number of packages have, at various times, been mislaid and lost. As it is impossible for the Captain or Agent to answer for any packages lost or mislaid whilst the present system continues, passengers are informed that, for the safety of their luggage and their better conveyance to shore, four large flag boats shall regularly attend, and any luggage being mislaid for the future, the boats and boatmen being known, will enable the proprietors to trace and find it out; and for avoiding further confusion, no boatman shall be allowed to come on board, but shall remain in their boats and take the passengers, with whatever luggage that shall be handed to them.

was eagerly sought when this was put out to contract, as it ensured a profitable return which financially assisted the winter services when passengers were few. Larger and faster vessels were built to put up the optimum case for the allocation of a mail contract and in doing so helped to 'improve the breed' not only for cross-channel steamers but also for the network of steamers engaged by the mid-19th century on cargo and passenger services around the coasts of Britain and Europe.

One of the great advantages of travel by paddle-propelled cargo and freight steamers was that livestock could be moved greater distances without great distress or loss of life, although it must be admitted that conditions were far from ideal and much overcrowding took place. Farm produce could also be moved from area to area or from one country to another, together with the increasing industrial products from factories. It has been quite correctly stated that the wealth of Britain in the 19th century was due to the exploitation of the British Empire. But a major contributory factor was the ease of communication provided by steam during the aptly named 'Industrial Revolution' and it was both the short and long-distance paddle steamers that provided the main form of marine transportation during this period.

Much of the same milieu accounted for the rapid expansion of coastal services in Europe and the great river routes of Australia and America, where even greater distances were involved. In Australia and America, the river paddle steamers were often responsible for providing the only means of sustaining the settlements

IDA

The iron paddle steamer *Ida* of 172 gross tons had been built in 1867 for use as a river steamer between Waterford and New Ross. Made redundant in 1904 by the extension of the railway to Waterford, she was laid up awaiting a purchaser. None was forthcoming and in 1908 the Bristol shipbreaker John Hurley acquired the vessel for scrapping. *Ida* was dismantled at Clevedon Pill where this photograph was taken.

rapidly growing in their interior regions. Besides bringing much needed provisions and stores, the river paddlers returned with the result of the settlers' labour and cultivation to be sold or stored at the larger towns or ports.

Fortunes were made and lost by the independent owners, but as in Britain, it was eventually the well-run and financially sound companies which largely took over from the private owner. Many of the well-known shipping concerns of today owed their origin to the ubiquitous paddle steamer.

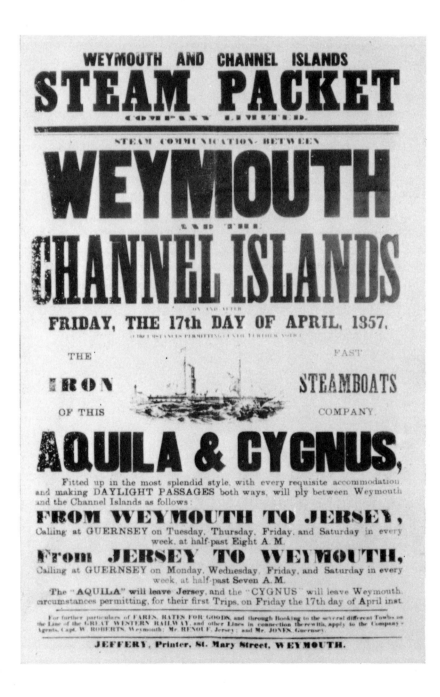

ROUEN and PARIS

The Paris Exhibition of 1889 was responsible for increased passenger traffic on the Newhaven to Dieppe service and the final pair of paddle-propelled vessels constructed for this route entered service the previous year in time to 'shake down' for the Exhibition trade. Both vessels held passenger certificates for 706 passengers and were fitted with compound diagonal engines which gave them a speed of almost 20 knots. An unusual feature of their design was the fact that they did not feature a navigating bridge, the wheel house being situated on the promenade deck, a portion of which was left free of passengers when entering or leaving port.

Both vessels served the Newhaven route for a number of years, the *Rouen* being sold for further service in 1903 and the *Paris* being finally withdrawn in 1912.

The photograph shows the graceful *Paris* leaving Newhaven Harbour for Dieppe with her steam winch still operating on her foredeck.

PARIS

The turtle-shaped foredeck and raked funnels of the *Paris* are shown to their best advantage in this picture of her alongside the quay at Newhaven.

S.S. Empress Queen, I.O.M.

EMPRESS QUEEN

The year 1897 saw the maiden voyage of the largest and fastest British cross-channel steamer ever built. Constructed by Fairfields of Glasgow and named appropriately *Empress Queen* in the year of Queen Victoria's Diamond Jubilee, her gross tonnage was 2,140 and she was capable of a speed exceeding 21½ knots.

As an excursion steamer she often carried over 2,000 passengers. It was said that her paddle wheels were the heaviest ever placed in a paddle steamer each weighing with the shaft over 70 tons. Her principal service was for the Isle of Man Steam Packet Company between Liverpool and Douglas. During the 1914–18 conflict, she was requisitioned by the Admiralty as a troop transport between England and France and whilst on passage on the 1st February, 1916, from Southampton in a thick fog, she struck Bembridge Ledge off the Isle of Wight. Although many attempts at salvage were made all were unsuccessful and she became a total loss.

Here the *Empress Queen* leaves Douglas for Liverpool in this official company postcard.

KONINGIN WILHELMINA

In 1895 the British shipbuilders of Fairfield and Company, Glasgow, delivered the last of a trio of cross-channel paddlers ordered by the Stoomvaart Maatschappij Company of Zeeland. The *Koningin Wilhelmina* was of 1,947 gross tons and powered by triple diagonal machinery developing 1,350 nautical horse power which gave her a speed of over 20 knots.

In 1910, following the introduction of screw vessels, all three ships were transferred to night services between Holland and Britain for which their smooth running was well suited. Following the outbreak of war, passenger services were withdrawn. Whilst on unknown duties on the 31st July, 1916, the *Koningin Wilhelmina* foundered, following an explosion by mine or torpedo.

Of the two other remaining ships of the trio, the *Koningin Regentes* was torpedoed whilst on passage to Britain with troops on the 8th June, 1918, and the *Prins Hendrik*, having survived the war, was sold for scrap in 1922.

AU REVOIR

The paddler *Au Revoir*, originally *Calais*, was one of three sister ships built in 1896 by Dennys of Dumbarton for the continental night services of the London, Chatham and Dover Railway. After a life of only fifteen years, the 979 gross tons vessels were sold having been made obsolete by the introduction of faster turbine steamers. The *Calais* was purchased by Monsieur P. Hattemer of Boulogne and sailed under the French flag from that port as a tender and excursion steamer. During the Great War she was torpedoed and sunk on the 26th February, 1916.

Although at first glance the *Au Revoir* seems to be leaving Boulogne, she is in fact entering the narrow harbour entrance by going astern with a stiff on-shore wind to assist her.

BALMORAL

With her decks crowded with passengers from Southampton and the Isle of Wight the *Balmoral* is seen arriving at Bournemouth about 1931. Constructed in 1900 this vessel undertook many long day excursions and was capable of 20 knots.

RED FUNNEL STEAMERS

GO ABROAD *for the day*

Special Excursions
by the P.S. "Balmoral"
(Weather and circumstances permitting)
from
Isle of Wight Piers
to

FRANCE (Cherbourg)

JULY 2nd—30th, inclusive

TUESDAYS, 2nd and 30th **WEDNESDAYS,** 10th and 24th	**To FRANCE** (Cherbourg) Leaving Sandown 9.25 ; Shanklin 9.40 a.m. Returning from Cherbourg 4.15 p.m. (English Time).
SUNDAY, 28th	**To FRANCE** (Cherbourg) Leaving Sandown 10.10 ; Shanklin 10.25 a.m. Returning from Cherbourg 4.15 p.m. (English Time).

LATEST DANCE AND ORCHESTRAL MUSIC PROVIDED ON BOARD

By arrangement with the French Government, passengers to Cherbourg by the P.S. "BALMORAL" will not require passports, but identity cards will be given in lieu thereof, and the particulars required must be filled in by the passenger before arriving at Cherbourg. Only British subjects or French subjects resident in this country will be permitted to embark, and under no circumstances will luggage be allowed.

RETURN FARE 12/6

(Including Landing Tax and Pier Tolls at Sandown and Shanklin).

Children between three and fourteen years are charged at Half Fare.

The Company reserve the right to alter the advertised times or withdraw any of the above sailings as weather and other circumstances may require.

The Company will not be liable for unavoidable delays, accidents, personal injury, or sea risks of any kind whatsoever. Neither will the Company be responsible for the loss of, or damage to, any passenger's luggage while using or being upon any Pier not belonging to the Company, whether or not the Toll in respect of the use of such Pier is included in the Fare.

Tickets will not be issued in excess of the number of passengers the vessel is allowed to carry under the Regulations of the Board of Trade.

The steamer is equipped with a large, well-appointed Dining Saloon, where Meals and Refreshments can be obtained, and the Catering undertaken by the Company is unsurpassed for quality and moderation in price.

Southampton, Isle of Wight and South of England Royal Mail Steam Packet Company Limited.

Printed by Southern Newspapers, Limited, 45, Above Bar, Southampton

4 The Rise of the Excursion Trade

It would be invidious to mention any particular, individual company or vessel during the expansive period of the British excursion steamer which occurred from the mid-19th century onwards and was only arrested by the outbreak of the First World War.

Whilst we must in no way belittle the progress and improvement in engineering standards achieved during this period, it was the demand brought about by social changes that had a great bearing on the design of the excursion steamer. At first, steam was the great experience of the time, just as flying and space travel have been during the 20th century. People flocked to see the 'new' steamboats and were attracted on board by the sheer novelty of this method of travel. It was not long before enterprising owners realised the great commercial potential of their ships and the more successful were able to add new tonnage and routes.

From the very early days of the steamship, operators had realised that the potential for increased profits was enormous if visitors and holiday-makers could be persuaded on board. Invariably their advertisements carried extravagant claims as to the speed and comfort of their respective vessels and even obsolete and often outclassed paddlers were described as 'elegant and commodious' or 'the fastest and most luxurious steamship on the station'.

The railways, once they had been accepted as a safe and reasonably comfortable means of travel, brought their loads of chattering passengers for a day out or for holidays which began to be provided for the middle classes. Thus, the excursion potential was provided at a most opportune time for steamship owners.

From about 1870, development of seaside resorts and the building of their piers gave opportunities for marine excursions to be expanded and the paddle steamer operators found themselves in the midst of a growth industry in travel and holidays. The only adverse factor that many of them had to contend with was competition, which often resulted in savage price cutting and drove a number of independent owners to bankruptcy. Companies which were founded on more substantial finance were able to absorb their smaller rivals and continued to provide well thought out and extensive sailing schedules, until they in turn were overcome by other factors in the mid-20th century.

The railway companies too were quick to realise that paddle steamers could provide an efficient means of transportation across water from one railhead to another, particularly amongst the lochs and rivers of Scotland. Combined rail and water excursions were extensively billed and in competing against each other the rival railways did much to promote the development and comfort of the ships.

By 1900 the main framework of paddle excursions had been well established, and there was hardly any seaside resort of size that did not boast of an excursion programme. River trips were also popular for those who had neither the time nor the inclination to visit the seaside and the railways provided fleets of attractive paddlers which could be used for communication or excursions.

Side by side with their British counterparts the paddle steamers of Europe and America became the mainstay of the nautically minded traveller and it was only the development of the internal combustion engine, coupled with later economic factors, which was to upset this equilibrium.

CARISBROOKE

Due to expansion of trade between Southampton and the Isle of Wight two similar vessels, the *Carisbrooke* and *Prince Leopold*, were delivered in 1876.

In November 1905 the *Carisbrooke* was sold to the Colwyn Bay and Liverpool Steamship Company for excursions along the North Wales Coast and named *Rhos Trevor*. Two years later she transferred to the Mersey Trading Company and in 1909 became the property of the Liverpool and North Wales Steamship Company, this time under the title of *St. Trillo*.

After service as a minesweeper she returned to the Welsh coast in 1919. On the 14th July, 1921, she ran aground whilst returning from a cruise to Caernarvon. Heeling over, there was some confusion among her 200 passengers but her Master, Captain Duffy, reassured them and they were transferred to motor boats. The paddle steamers *Snowdon* and *Greyhound* came to the rescue. On the rising tide the vessel slipped off the rocks into deeper water. The ship's cook fell overboard but was rescued by the efforts of another member of the crew. Under her own power the *St. Trillo* sailed to Port Dinonwic.

Following the accident, her owners decided to dispose of the vessel, and she was purchased by a Spanish shipowner, the Marquis de Olaso. After further service in Spain her hull was converted into sleeping accommodation for duck shooting parties, her name remaining on Lloyds' Register until 1931-2.

The illustration shows the former Southampton steamer *Carisbrooke* as the *St. Trillo* whilst in the service of the Liverpool and North Wales Steamship Company.

The navigating bridge and paddle box of the *Carisbrooke* shortly after her transfer from the South Coast.

LORD MORTON

The popularity of the Galloway steamers was in no doubt when this photograph of the *Lord Morton* was taken on a fine August Sunday in 1911. The black tops to the company's ships were added about this time. To the left of the *Lord Morton* lies the paddle tug *Fifeshire*.

LORD MORTON

When built by S. and H. Morton of Leith in 1883 for the Galloway Steam Packet Company, the *Lord Morton* was unusual in having both funnels situated forward of her paddle boxes and only a single diagonal engine. The vessel is seen unloading passengers at the Quay in preference to the Pier at Aberdour about 1900.

In April 1918 she was purchased by the Admiralty and fitted out as a hospital ship and sent in company with two other paddle steamers to the White Sea. Unfortunately, owing to an engine defect she was unable to return to the United Kingdom and the 220 gross tons vessel was destroyed by British troops to prevent her falling into the hands of the Bolsheviks.

LORNA DOONE

By 1890 competition from the Campbell fleet in the Bristol Channel was intense, and Edwards, Robertson and Company attempted to meet the threat by ordering a new vessel of some 410 gross tons from the Clyde shipyard of Napier, Shanks and Bell. Delivered the following year and named *Lorna Doone*, she proved a valuable unit but in 1896 the company's vessels were sold to a Mr. John Gunn of Cardiff. Two years later he received an approach from the South Coast to charter the vessel. Seeing the chance of a useful profit, Gunn declined to lease or charter but informed the Southampton, Isle of Wight and South of England Royal Mail Steam Packet Company that he was willing to sell the vessel. Passing to their ownership, *Lorna Doone* was a stopgap to meet further Campbell expansion at Southampton, strangely enough the same company which had provided opposition to her original owner when she had been built.

The photograph shows *Lorna Doone* at Lundy Island in the Bristol Channel where passengers had to be landed by rowing boat, a long and tedious affair when the ship had a full complement of passengers as shown here.

LORNA DOONE

When serving from Southampton the ex-Bristol Channel paddler *Lorna Doone* underwent several changes of profile. In this photograph taken in the late 1930's she lies at the Royal Pier Southampton on an early summer morning awaiting her turn to take passengers to the Isle of Wight.

The saloon and bar of the Southampton based *Lorna Doone* resplendent in a coat of
new paint at the beginning of yet another excursion season in the mid-1930's.

P.S. "RAVENSWOOD"   P. & A. CAMPBELL, Ltd.

RAVENSWOOD

The *Ravenswood* of 1891 underwent a drastic change of profile during her service with the White Funnel Fleet of P. and A. Campbell. When delivered from the yard of S. McKnight and Company at Ayr she emerged with twin funnels, bridge behind her funnels, square posts to her saloons and a well-balanced paddle-box of traditional design.

During the course of sixty-four years service each of these features was changed, so that the *Ravenswood* of the 1950's could scarcely be recognised as that of the 1890's. During a post-war refit at Hills of Bristol in 1946, she was fitted with concealed paddle-boxes almost as if the old lady was ashamed of being a paddler. This type of box was also fitted to the two post-war paddle vessels built for Campbells, but although perhaps more streamlined and in keeping with the post-war age, they added nothing to the general appearance of the ships and were prone to water clogging in heavy seas.

The *Ravenswood* was withdrawn after the 1955 season and left Bristol for the ship-breakers at Newport on the 20th October, 1955.

P. & A. Campbell's Bristol Channel Passenger Steamers.

ON BOARD P. S. "RAVENSWOOD.

RAVENSWOOD

The old and the new. The top photograph shows the traditional fan-shaped box of *Ravenswood* on the 30th September, 1939, whilst laid up prior to a second spell of war service.

Below is her modernised box on the 13th April, 1946, prior to re-entering passenger service on the Bristol Channel.

KOH-I-NOOR

This composite postcard of the *Koh-i-Noor* is a typical example of the type of Edwardian postcard sold on board pleasure steamers and at their ports of call.

In 1892 the Victoria Steamboat Association of London placed an order for a twin-funnelled, one-masted paddler from the Fairfield Shipbuilding Company, to be employed in running excursions down the Thames. On her trials she attained 19.499 knots powered by a fine set of compound diagonal engines. Her name signified that her owners intended the ship to be a 'jewel of the Thames' as she was named after the well-known diamond presented to Queen Victoria in 1850 on the annexation of the Punjab.

Koh-i-Noor nearly became a nautical casualty on her delivery voyage. Whilst steaming south on the night of the 26th May off the Welsh coast, she stranded on Porthgain Rock off St. David's Head sustaining considerable damage to her bow. After backing off she proceeded for temporary repairs at Milford Haven and placed on the grid-iron at Neyland. Returning to her builders on the Clyde, she was fitted with a completely new bow section in six days and eventually the steamer arrived in London on the 2nd July, 1892, ready to take up her duties on the following day.

The *Koh-i-Noor* soon became a popular vessel running from London's Old Swan Pier to Southend, Clacton and occasionally to Harwich. Later her service was shortened to the Thanet resorts and for a number of years she was the Saturday 'Husbands' Boat' to Margate and Ramsgate, so called as it was usual for husbands to travel from London at weekends to visit their wives and families spending their holidays at these resorts.

By 1914 she was in need of re-boilering and had sailed for the Clyde shortly before the outbreak of war. The work was not carried out and *Koh-i-Noor* was laid up for the duration in the Gareloch where she remained until 1918 when she was sold for £6,200 for breaking up, being cut up at Morecambe in 1919.

Crowded with passengers the *Royal Sovereign* is shown leaving Margate at the start of another excursion.

Whilst under the ownership of the General Steam Navigation Company, the *Royal Sovereign* left London Bridge at 9 a.m. and arrived at Margate 3¾ hours later, the trip to Ramsgate taking a further 45 minutes with only a 5-minute turnround before commencing the return journey. This sailing bill dates from 1929, her last season on the Thames.

ROYAL SOVEREIGN

Such was the immediate success of the *Koh-i-Noor* that the Fairfield Company who had a strong financial interest in the Victoria Steamboat Association, ordered an additional ship in 1893. Named *Royal Sovereign*, her general arrangement was very similar to that of her predecessor except in the positioning of the funnels which in the later ship were spaced further apart. Both ships were fitted with electric light, a post office, hairdressers, two bathrooms, book and fruit stalls.

The *Royal Sovereign* ran in consort with the *Koh-i-Noor* to Margate and Ramsgate, both ships becoming a popular part of the Thameside scene. The *Royal Sovereign* was re-boilered in 1909 but not impressed for Admiralty service during the 1914–18 war. Instead, she was laid up at Tilbury Docks, and in 1918 sold for £8,300 to a new company formed for the express purpose of running the vessel on her previous routes.

After eleven more years of service the company sold out to the General Steam Navigation Company who ran her fifty-six times between London and Margate. The company evidently found the ageing ship too expensive to run and in February 1930 she was sold for £3,500 to the Dutch shipbreaker T. G. Pas of Nieuw Lekkerland.

LA MARGUERITE

Following the *Koh-i-Noor* and *Royal Sovereign*, Mr. A. E. Williams, the manager of the Victoria Steamboat Association, suggested that it would be possible to run a regular service to Boulogne on the French coast and back to London again on a daily basis.

Accordingly Fairfields constructed *La Marguerite*, named after Mr. Williams' daughter, the new paddler being some 5 knots faster than the other ships of the Association. As she was too large and fast for the Thames Conservancy, her departure was made from Tilbury calling at Margate before crossing the Channel. The London, Tilbury and Southend Railway ran a special train from Fenchurch Street Station to connect at Tilbury and for the first time the London public had a cross-channel service for pleasure or business.

Unfortunately *La Marguerite* proved an expensive vessel to maintain and after the initial excitement had worn off, passenger receipts were not all that could be desired.

In 1904, the largest of the Thames paddle steamer fleet was sold to the Liverpool and North Wales Steamship Company who ran her on the Liverpool, Llandudno and Menai Bridge service. In March 1915 she was impressed into Admiralty service as a troop transport between Southampton and various French ports and it is said she steamed 52,000 miles with over 360,000 troops, in this rôle.

Released in April 1919, she was chartered by the Isle of Man Steam Packet Company who had lost a similar sized paddle steamer, the *Empress Queen*, on war service. During the following year she returned to service from Liverpool being finally withdrawn and sold for scrapping after her final voyage on the 28th September, 1925.

LA MARGUERITE

La Marguerite whilst on service with the Liverpool and North Wales Steamship Company approaches Liverpool.

MINERVA

The *Minerva* and her sister ship *Glen Rosa* were both constructed in 1893 for the fleet of the Glasgow and South Western Railway Company. They were of 306 gross tons and built by J. and G. Thomson at Clydebank, and were unusual in that their fore-castle extended half way to their bows at the level of the main promenade deck. This design feature not being repeated in subsequent vessels. A third vessel of the same design named *Slieve Donard* was built for Irish waters and later became the Campbell steamer *Albion*.

The *Minerva* was an auxiliary patrol vessel during the 1914–18 war, being stationed for a time at Malta. She did not return to Scotland being sold to Turkish owners and broken up about 1927.

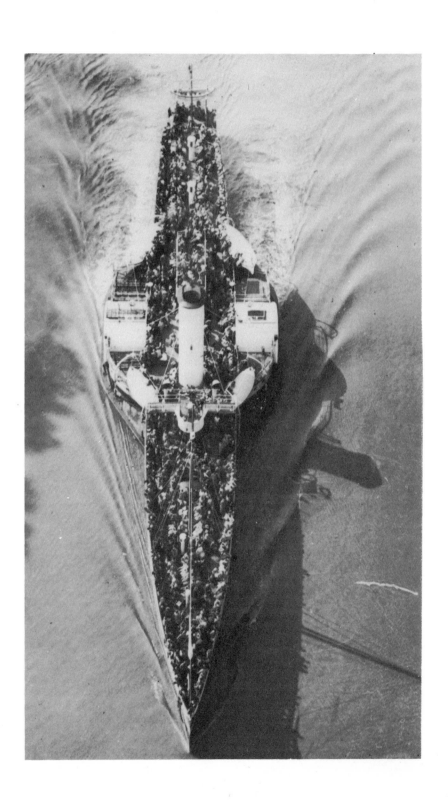

BRITANNIA

The flagship of the P. and A. Campbell paddle steamer fleet which operated in the Bristol Channel, the *Britannia* was constructed for the company in 1896 by McKnight of Ayr and fitted with diagonal compound engines by Hutson and Son of Glasgow. She was a direct development of the *Westward Ho*, built two years previously, which was the first excursion steamer south of the Clyde to have the promenade deck extended to the stern.

The Campbell steamers were more popularly known as 'The White Funnel Fleet' and their *Britannia* served in the Bristol Channel, and, when the company extended its service to the English Channel, from Brighton, Eastbourne and other Sussex Piers. From the 5th February, 1915, to the 8th April, 1919, she was operated by the British Admiralty as a minesweeper, being returned to Glasgow for refitting on the latter date.

Like many other excursion steamers her appearance changed. Originally fitted with a tall single funnel and square ports to her lounge and forward deck, she was later fitted with more practical round ports and a cowl top fitted to her inner funnel casing. In 1935 she acquired a large and more modern elliptical funnel together with a deckhouse over the main companionway aft of her paddle boxes. Yet a further change occurred after further war service during 1939–45 when she emerged resplendent with two funnels but minus her deckhouse.

After sixty years of service *Britannia* left Cardiff on the 7th December, 1956, to be broken up at Newport, South Wales. It has been estimated that she steamed over half a million miles and carried over 1,250,000 passengers.

Some of the crew of *Britannia* caught during an off duty moment on the 12th May, 1913.

This unusual shot was taken as the *Britannia* passed under the Clifton Suspension Bridge near Bristol on the 1st August, 1938.

TALISMAN

Unlike the vessel of the same name which replaced her in 1935, the first vessel of the name was a typical Clyde paddler of the 1890's powered by a single cylinder diagonal engine. Launched on the 30th March, 1896, by A. and J. Inglis she entered service on the Rothesay and Kyles of Bute run for the North British Railway.

During the 1914–18 war she was employed on minesweeping from Troon and later from Portsmouth as *H.M.S. Talla* returning from the Clyde on the 26th February, 1919. Before re-entering passenger service her fore-saloon which previously had alleyways around it, was extended to the full width of her hull, and, in common with more modern practice, her bridge was placed in front of the funnel. *Talisman* remained on the service for which she was built until broken up in 1934 at Barrow.

SNOWDON

The Snowdon Passenger Steamship Company was formed in 1892 by Mr. W. H. Dodd who had previously run two tugs on excursion work along the North Wales coastline. This handsome two-funnelled saloon vessel was delivered by Lairds of Birkenhead in the same year.

Snowdon had a certificate for 462 passengers and a gross tonnage of 338. She was impressed as a minesweeper during the 1914–18 war, returning to passenger service in 1919, and was finally scrapped at Port Glasgow in 1931.

The "Worthing Belle" leaving Brighton Pier.

WORTHING BELLE

The *Worthing Belle* was a product of Barclay Curle in 1885 for the North British Railway and had run from Craigendoran under the name of *Diana Vernon*. In 1901 she was purchased by Captain J. Lee who had been connected with running paddle steamers along the Sussex coast for a number of years. She was renamed the *Worthing Belle*. She entered service on the 4th April and ran under Lee's ownership until 1913 under the command of Captain William Trenance.

Sold in March 1914 to the Administration de Navires a Vapeur Ottomane, she was renamed the *Touzla* and used for ferry service on the Bosphorus.

Edwardian sailing bill

Members of the crew of the ex-cross-channel paddle steamer *Brighton* pose for the camera whilst the vessel lies at Ilfracombe under the ownership of Pockett's Bristol Channel Steam Packet Company.

BRIGHTON

The Pockett cross-channel steamer *Brighton* off Lynmouth awaits her passengers
which have been ferried ashore by rowing boats, an operation which is still carried
out from Bristol Channel excursion steamers today.

GLEN ROSA

The elegance of a Victorian Pier is exemplified by this postcard of Hastings Pier and
Pavilion, with the paddle steamer *Glen Rosa* just about to depart at 4 p.m. during the
season of 1906.

WEEROONA

Sailing into the distance of Port Philip Bay is this fine example of an Australian excursion steamer. She is the *Weeroona* built in Scotland during 1910 by A. and J. Inglis for the Melbourne Bay Steamers Ltd.

The *Weeroona* saw service in the Philippines during the Second World War as a Recreation Ship for the United States Navy between 1941 and 1945. Restored to passenger service, she was eventually withdrawn and scrapped in July 1954.

ERINS ISLE

On the 12th June, 1912, the Scottish shipbuilding yard of A. and J. Inglis, builders of many British excursion steamers, launched the *Erins Isle*, a fine steamer with her promenade deck extending the full length of her hull. She was the first vessel of this type owned by the Belfast and County Down Railway Company.

For £3 3s. 0d. (£3.15) the intending passenger from Bristol or Cardiff could in 1911 have a four-day trip to Spithead and back to witness the Naval Review and illuminations held in honour of the Coronation of King George V. Several alternatives were available, such as returning by train or an extra day at Bournemouth, embarking on another of the company's steamers on the following day. It is to be hoped that neither vessel was crowded to capacity as no sleeping berths were provided on either vessel!

Southern and Great Western Railways and P. & A. Campbell Ltd.

SPECIAL EXCURSION

From Brighton, Worthing, Eastbourne & Hastings

TO ILFRACOMBE, CARDIFF & BRISTOL

(Weather and circumstances permitting), by the Magnificent Saloon Steamer

"DEVONIA"

On Thursday, Sept. 29th, 1927

Leaving BRIGHTON (Palace Pier) at 11.30 a.m., due to arrive at Ilfracombe about noon on Friday, Sept. 30th, leaving 4.30 p.m for Cardiff, arrive 7.0 p.m., Bristol about 8.45 p.m.

Single Fare for the Steamer 15/- (Tickets on Board).

Return Fares to ILFRACOMBE, CARDIFF, BRISTOL

				OUT BY BOAT HOME BY RAIL.
From BRIGHTON	40/-	35/-	30/-	Passengers from
„ WORTHING	40/-	36/6	31/-	Worthing, Eastbourne
„ EASTBOURNE	49/6	42/-	37/-	and Hastings join the
„ HASTINGS	51/6	44/6	40/-	Steamer at Brighton Palace Pier.

The journeys from Bristol and Cardiff to Brighton may be made either via London or Salisbury. From Ilfracombe by the Salisbury and Southern Co. route only. Those to Eastbourne and Hastings via London only. Those to Worthing via the Salisbury and Southern Co. route only.

Tickets may be obtained in advance from Messrs. T. Cook & Son, 81 King's Rd., Brighton, or at the Southern Railway Company's Booking Offices, Brighton, Worthing, Eastbourne and Hastings, available to return by any train carrying third-class passengers, up to and including October 16th by the routes specified above.

Full particulars from Agents of P. & A. CAMPBELL Ltd.

W. REID, 15 Ship Street, Brighton.   Telegrams : "Ravenswood, Brighton."   Telephone : 5478 Brighton.
W. A. PELLY, Pier, Eastbourne.   Telegrams : "Pier, Eastbourne."   Telephone : 1690 Eastbourne.
F. L. PHILLIPS, Pier, Hastings.   Telegrams : "Pier, Hastings."   Telephone : 1032 Hastings.

The Cliftonville Press Co. Ltd. 119 Blatchington Road, Hove

GRAND STEAMER TRIPS

BY SALOON STEAMER

QUEEN OF THE SOUTH

CAPT. HECTOR McFADYEN (late of "Brighton Queen")

WEATHER AND CIRCUMSTANCES PERMITTING.

MUSIC AND DANCING ON BOARD.

SPECIAL BENEFIT WEEK.

One-fifth of the total Fares will be divided equally between the Crew and Staffs of the Palace and West Piers on all Sailings from Monday, October 1st, until Sunday, October 7th, 1923, inclusive.

SATURDAY, SEPTEMBER 29.—**Morning Trip off Newhaven,** viewing Departure of French Mail Boat, leaving West Pier 11, Palace Pier 11.15, back 12.45. Fare 2/-

Afternoon Trip off Beachy Head Lighthouse, leaving West Pier 3, Palace Pier 3.15, back 5.30. Fare 2/-

SUNDAY, SEPTEMBER 30.—**Morning Trip in the English Channel,** leaving West Pier 11 10, Palace Pier 11.20, back 12.45. Fare 2/-

Afternoon Trip to Worthing, allowing one hour ashore, leaving Palace Pier 3, West Pier 3 15, return from Worthing 5.10, back 6. Fares 1/6 single, 2/- return, or to include Trip out of Worthing, 2/6

MONDAY, OCTOBER 1.—**Morning Trip past Peacehaven, Seaford, etc.,** leaving West Pier 11, Palace Pier 11.15, back 12.45. Fare 2/-

Afternoon Trip to Newhaven, to view arrival of French Mail Boat from Dieppe, leaving West Pier 3, Palace Pier 3.15; return from Newhaven 5. Fare 2/- return, 1/6 single.

TUESDAY, OCTOBER 2.—**Morning Trip to Beachy Head Lighthouse,** leaving West P. 11, Palace P. 11.15, back 12.45. Fare 2/-

Afternoon Trip to Newhaven, allowing 1 hour ashore, leaving West P. 3, Palace P. 3.15; return from Newhaven 5, back 5.45. Fares: 1/6 Single, 2/- Return.

WEDNESDAY, OCTOBER 3.—**Morning Cruise Westward towards Littlehampton,** passing Shoreham, etc., leaving Palace P. 11, West P. 11.15, back 12.45. Fare 2/-

Afternoon Trip to Beachy Head Lighthouse, leaving West P. 3, Palace P. 3.15, back 5.30. Fare 2/-

THURSDAY, OCTOBER 4.—**Morning Cruise in the English Channel to View the Shipping,** leaving West P. 11, Palace P. 11.15, back 12.45. Fare 2/-

Afternoon Trip to Newhaven, allowing 1 hour ashore, leaving West P. 3, Palace P. 3.15; return from Newhaven 5, back 5.45. Fares: 1/6 Single, 2/- Return.

FRIDAY, OCTOBER 5.—**Morning Cruise past Newhaven Harbour to see Departure of French Mail Boat,** leaving West P. 11, Palace P. 11.15, back 12.45. Fare 2/-

Afternoon Trip off Beachy Head Lighthouse, passing Peacehaven, Seven Sisters, etc. leaving West P. 3, Palace P. 3.15, back 5.30. Fare 2/-

SATURDAY, OCTOBER 6.—**Cruise in the English Channel,** leaving West P. 11, Palace P. 11.15, back 12.45. Fare 2/-

Afternoon Trip off Littlehampton and Bognor, leaving Palace P. 3, West P. 3.15, back 5.30. Fare 2/-

SUNDAY, OCTOBER 7.—**Morning Trip to Beachy Head Lighthouse,** leaving West P. 11.10, Palace P. 11.20, back 12.45. Fare 2/-

Afternoon Trip to Newhaven Harbour, allowing 1 hour ashore, to view Arrival of French Mail Steamer, leaving West P. 3, Palace P. 3.15; return from Newhaven 5, back 5.45. Fares: 1/6 Single, 2/- Return.

| Children half-price. Minimum fare 1/- | This Vessel is fitted with Wireless, and passengers can hear all the news and concerts sent out from the Marconi Stations. |

Refreshments of the Best Quality at Popular Prices.

SPECIAL PARTIES CATERED FOR

All passengers are carried subject to the conditions printed on the back of all tickets issued. The Company reserve the right to cancel all or any of the above advertised Sailings without notice.

By Order of CHANNEL EXCURSION STEAMERS, Ltd.

Tel. : **138 Brighton.**
E. & S. Ld.

Office—**PALACE PIER, BRIGHTON**
H. H. BROWN, *Managing Director and Secretary*

In Scotland between the wars the excursion season began to run down three or four weeks sooner than those in the English Channel. This sailing bill of early September 1928 shows the final excursions performed by the London Midland and Scottish Railway steamer *Juno* before being laid up for the winter.

QUEEN OF THE SOUTH

Due to war losses P. and A. Campbell were unable to re-open excursion services along the Sussex coast until 1923. In the previous year a short-lived concern called Channel Excursions Ltd. purchased the *Woolwich Belle* of 1891 in an attempt to fill the void presented by the Campbell absence and to get a foothold on the station. The *Woolwich Belle* renamed *Queen of the South* operated a number of short excursions in 1922 and 1923 but was unable to compete against the three Campbell steamers which had returned during the latter season.

This sailing bill of the last excursions by *Queen of the South* from Brighton is interesting in two respects. It shows she was commanded by Captain Hector McFadyen who had charge of Campbell's *Brighton Queen* before the war and that some of the proceeds of the last week of sailings were devoted for the crew's benefit.

In 1924 the *Queen of the South* was sold to the New Medway Steam Packet Company with whom she sailed until scrapped in 1932.

Local photographers were never slow to appreciate the custom resulting from the sea of smiling faces provided by day-trippers. In these photographs, passengers are just about to set out from Ilfracombe on board the Campbell steamer *Cambria* on the 30th August, 1929, and from Bournemouth in the Cosens paddler *Victoria* on the 30th May, 1928.

The Master of the *Royal Eagle* was Captain 'Bill' Branthwaite, generally regarded as a magnificent seaman who ruled his ship and all aboard her with a firm yet benevolent hand.

ROYAL EAGLE

The size and splendour of the pride of the London steamers during the 1930's, the *Royal Eagle* is shown in these postcards sold on board.

BOURNEMOUTH QUEEN

The sartorial splendour of an Edwardian-built paddle steamer. Pictured in the 1930's, the saloon of the *Bournemouth Queen* of 1908 complete with builders' model (left) and mosquito netting, seldom needed during an English summer, together with flowers, gives a fine example of the care and elegance provided for passengers.

Saturday evening cruise

SATURDAY, 7th JULY, 1923

Evening Trip to the Isle of Wight
(Weather and circumstances permitting)

by the s.s.

"BOURNEMOUTH QUEEN"

GRAND EVENING CRUISE

to

YARMOUTH

Passing the Needles, Alum Bay, Totland Bay, etc.

accompanied by the
BOSCOMBE SILVER PRIZE BAND
OF 22 PERFORMERS

Leaving Bournemouth Pier 6.30 p.m.   Returning from Yarmouth 7.40 p.m.
Back about 9.0 p.m.

Special **2/-** Fare

Further particulars can be obtained of
The Southampton, Isle of Wight and South of England Royal Mail Steam Packet Company, Ltd.
L. T. WILKINS, Director and Manager, Western Esplanade, Southampton, and
F. VENNER, Observer Chambers, Albert Road, Bournemouth.   Tel. No. 1062

Richmond Printeries, Bournemouth 21/6/23

BOURNEMOUTH QUEEN

Extensively rebuilt after her service in the Second World War the *Bournemouth Queen* emerged with a handsome profile which included a fatter funnel, covered wheelhouse and canvas dodgers to protect those on her foredeck. She is seen here leaving Swanage Bay for Bournemouth Pier in 1947.

When withdrawn from Bournemouth in 1950 she subsequently operated from Southampton for another seven years. In December 1957, forty-nine years after her launch, she was towed to Ghent to be broken up by Belgian breakers.

 The twenty-four-strong crew of the *Bournemouth Queen* pose at Southampton about 1935.

The assembly of warships at Spithead for Royal occasions were always the source of additional revenue for excursion steamer operators who lost no opportunity to issue special bills to advertise the occasion. Such trips were always well patronised whatever the weather.

In 1935, on the occasion of the Silver Jubilee of King George V, the *Brighton Belle* and *Devonia* sailed from Brighton on Saturday, 26th July, neither ship returning until the early hours of the following day. The former vessel on this occasion was chartered by Thomas Cook and Sons, the well-known British travel company.

P. & A. CAMPBELL LTD.

SPITHEAD.

THE GREAT ASSEMBLY OF
250 WAR VESSELS.

MAGNIFICENT ILLUMINATIONS AND SEARCHLIGHT DISPLAY

IN THE EVENING.

SPECIAL AFTERNOON & EVENING EXCURSIONS

BY THE CROSS-CHANNEL STEAMERS,

DEVONIA & BRIGHTON BELLE

Well equipped with fine Saloons, and Catering a speciality.

SATURDAY, JULY 26th

The "**BRIGHTON BELLE**" leaves Brighton Palace Pier 2.45 p.m., West Pier 3 p.m. for a Cruise through the various lines of Warships, afterwards takes up her position to witness the Illuminations, then returning to Brighton. Back about 2 a.m.

Tickets obtained before the day, **8/6** ; on the day, **10/6**.

From Messrs. THOS. COOK & SON, 81, King's Road, Brighton, or at the Company's Office, 7, Old Steine, Brighton.

SATURDAY, JULY 26th
Evening Trip to Spithead to View the Illuminations.

The "**DEVONIA**" leaves Brighton Palace Pier 6.50 p.m., West Pier 7 p.m. and takes up her position in time to see the Marvellous Exhibition of 250 War Vessels Illuminated, then returning to Brighton. Back about 1.30 a.m. Fare **5** -

Full particulars may be obtained from P. & A. CAMPBELL Ltd., 7, Old Steine, Brighton. **W. REID**, Agent.

The Southern Publishing Co., Ltd., 130, North Street, Brighton. P8404.

COSENS & COMPANY, Ltd.

50 Commercial Road, Weymouth
STEAMERS: Embassy, Consul, etc.

Complimentary Pass

(Exclusive of all Pier Tolls)

Available for the month of...196......

No   1507

Pass..*and One.*

ORDINARY EXCURSION FROM BOURNEMOUTH

This Pass is to be shown when required, and delivered to the Collector at the end of the journey.

It is NOT AVAILABLE for any other Month, Bank Holidays, Motor Coach Tours, or any other Trips that may be specially notified.

To be used during the Month of issue only.

Sherren 621188/18 bks.

This Portion to be given up on the OUTWARD Journey

1507

No.

CONDITIONS UPON WHICH THIS FREE PASS IS GRANTED

This FREE PASS is granted by COSENS & COMPANY, LIMITED, on the following conditions of carriage :

(1) Passengers are carried subject to it being hereby agreed that Cosens & Co., Limited (hereinafter referred to as "the Company" which term shall include the Shipowners, the Line, Charterers, Managers, Operators and the Ship, as the case may be) shall not be liable for the death of or any injury, damage, loss, delay or accident to passengers, their apparel or baggage, whensoever, wheresoever and howsoever caused and whether by negligence of their servants or agents, or by unseaworthiness of the vessel (whether existing at the time of embarkation or sailing, or at any other time) or otherwise nor for any sea or river risks whatsoever.

(2) By accepting or receiving a ticket each passenger agrees both on his or her behalf and on behalf of any person or child travelling with him or her or in his or her care that all rights, exceptions from liability, defences and immunities of whatsoever nature referred to in Clause 1 hereof shall in all respects enure also for the benefit of any servants or agents of the Company acting in the course of or in connection with their employment so that in no circumstances shall any such servant or agent as the result of so acting be under any liability to any such passenger or to any such person or child greater than or different from that of the Company. For the purposes of the agreement contained in this clause, the Company is or shall be deemed to be acting on behalf and for the benefit of all persons who are or may be its servants or agents from time to time, and all such persons shall to this extent be or be deemed to be parties to the contract contained in or evidenced by such ticket.

QUEEN OF SOUTHEND

The *Queen of Southend* is seen here in unusual surroundings at Southampton on the 19th May, 1937. In common with several other excursion steamers from the Thames and Bristol Channel, she had ventured to the South Coast to undertake charter work in connection with the Coronation Naval Review of King George VI.

Side by side with the issue of season tickets, complimentary tickets and passes have always been available to share and bond holders of steamer companies. These were sometimes limited to sailings from a particular port or pier and not available for example on Bank Holidays or Special Excursions.

Complimentary passes were often issued for a monthly excursion on a single occasion to people who had benefited the company in some way, such as displaying a sailing bill on a hoarding or shop window. Those given by Cosens of Weymouth and used as late as 1963, were perhaps unusual in that a printers' block, supposedly depicting one of their paddle steamers, was the self same block used in newspaper advertisements during the 1890's.

MURRAY RIVER QUEEN

Perhaps the world's newest paddle excursion vessel, the *Murray River Queen* commenced sailing in 1974, being launched at Hindmarsh Island, Goolwa, Australia, during the previous year. She was the first vessel of any size to be built at Goolwa since 1913 and is driven by two diesel-engined side-mounted paddles. Like the *Coonawarra* she undertakes week-long journeys on the River Murray for the benefit of holidaymakers.

The *Murray River Queen* was constructed at a cost of 300,000 Australian dollars and has accommodation for 72 passengers with 36 cabins, each equipped with showers and toilets. Reservations being made through the South Australian Tourist Board.

Passing scores of riverside bungalows the *Murray River Queen* produces the typical wash of a paddler as she sails towards Morgan.

5 Ferries, River and Lake Steamers

Although always overshadowed by their more famous and glamorous relatives, the smaller paddle-driven ferries have earned their place in maritime history. It was realised that the regularity of steam-driven vessels could provide an adaptable timetable, tailor-made for summer and winter, providing a speedy way across estuary, river and lake.

In America, owing to the much greater distances involved, the ferry steamer tended to be much larger than its British counterpart; in fact, some of the largest paddle steamers ever employed in this rôle were operated between centres of population in the United States. On the continent of Europe, the rivers Danube, Rhine and Elbe saw regular services well established by 1840, carrying freight, livestock and passengers.

Some of the better-known paddle steamers of the world are those of the Mark Twain world of the mighty Mississippi. As elsewhere, the quest for speed was always predominant, being brought to a head in 1870 by the well-known race between the stern-wheelers *Robert E. Lee* and the *Natchez*. It is said that over a million dollars were staked on this race from New Orleans to St. Louis. When the victorious *Robert E. Lee* arrived, the race had taken three days, eighteen hours and fourteen minutes. The opening up of middle America, before the establishment of overland rail travel, was largely due to the wood-burning paddlers of the Ohio and Mississippi.

In Australia also, the river paddle steamer played its part in opening up communications between isolated settlements situated along the banks of rivers and waterways. The River Murray, sixty miles east of Adelaide, was the Australian equivalent of the Mississippi. Paddle steamers once plied over four thousand miles of the rivers and tributaries of the Darling–Murray Basin, visiting such outback ports as Wilcannia, Wahgunyah, Walgett and the colourful-sounding Wagga Wagga. Nor must their part in developing the wool trade be forgotten when, laden with Australia's principal export, they made their way downstream across the shallows and snags of their tortuous course.

By comparison, lake steamers seemed to lead a sheltered existence. In Europe, they still plod their way across the Swiss or Italian waters and may perhaps become the last bastions of paddle propulsion in the world. The lake steamers are now largely engaged on summer excursion work, their rôle as carriers of freight being superseded by motor transport and the railways. The majority have now been converted from steam to oil or other means of propulsion but fortunately many retain the traditional outward design of their predecessors.

The oldest paddle steamer in the world, the Norwegian *Skibladner*, built in 1856, still sails on Lake Mjosa taking twelve hours to cover the trip from Eidsvoll to Killehammer and return, whilst the British *Maid of the Loch*, nearly a hundred years her junior, provides a major tourist attraction of Loch Lomond.

The popular conception of an American river paddler is of a huge floating platform with three or four decks, propelled by immense paddle wheels usually located at the stern—the typical American 'Showboat'. In essence, the American river boats were developed by operational necessity rather than the need to provide a suitable 'movie' background. Most rivers in the United States are wide and shallow; thus the requirement for shallow draught was of even greater importance than that of Europe. In addition, landing stages were often no more than a wooden base on the river bank with little provision for loading cargo or passengers.

It is convenient to divide American paddlers into Eastern and Western derivatives. Eastern river steamboats were mainly employed on the Hudson between New York and Albany, inaugurated by Fulton with the *Clermont* in 1807. Further services were operated from New York to Long Island Sound. In the main, Eastern steamboats were side rather than stern-wheelers, much larger than their European contemporaries and often with a carrying capacity of over one thousand passengers.

The Western river steamboats were side-propelled on the lower reaches of such rivers as the Mississippi and fitted with a stern-wheel on tributaries where side-wheelers would have been too vulnerable. Besides forming an important means of communication and transportation, other uses included towage and the well-known 'Showboats' which developed from the need to provide entertainment for the townships and plantations, sometimes inaccessible to any other form of transport.

A peculiarity of American steamers was the use of wood as integral parts of the engine. In Europe, iron and steel was plentiful but in the middle of the 19th century these materials were not easily available to American shipbuilders. Consequently they turned to wood as a substitute, using it for engine frames, bedplates, paddle shaft frames and even on occasions for the connecting rod. Boiler pressures too were conceived to run at over a hundred pounds per square inch, whilst those in Britain and elsewhere were still being

EUREKA

The American paddle-propelled ferries have always been larger in tonnage and capacity than those of other parts of the world. The *Eureka*, a side-wheeler constructed in 1890, was no exception. Constructed of wood by the Northern Pacific Yard at Tiburon, California, her accommodation provided for 3,500 passengers with a gross tonnage of over 2,000. When built the claim was made that she was the fastest double-ended ferry boat in the world with a speed of 18 knots.

Originally named *Ukiah* she was operated by the San Francisco and North Pacific Railroad, later the Northwestern Pacific, employed between San Francisco and Tiburon. In 1920 she was extensively reconstructed and her passenger capacity reduced to 2,300 in order to provide space for 120 cars, and placed on a service from Hyde Street to Sausalits still across the San Francisco Bay. Some idea of the need and popularity for such large ferries can be gained from the fact that in 1930, the Southern Pacific Railroad and its subsidiaries, including the Northwestern Pacific, carried over 40 million passengers and operated a fleet of 30 vessels.

The *Eureka* was withdrawn from the Sausalits run in 1941 and transferred to the direct operation of the Southern Pacific who used her from Oakland to Mole-Ferry. Some twelve years later, she underwent another extensive rebuild, which should have given her many more years of service. This was not to be, however, as on the 10th February, 1957, her massive crank-pin snapped and economic repair was deemed impossible. Thus ended sixty-seven years of almost continuous passenger service at San Francisco. The vessel now forms part of the San Francisco Maritime Museum.

limited to about twenty p.s.i.

Besides the American river steamers, the paddle ferries of San Francisco have added their own colour to the history of the paddle steamer. The vessels were an integral part of the main-line railroad business carrying passengers, mail, baggage and general cargo including livestock. Before they were replaced by motorised trucks, specially trained horses were quartered on board to embark and disembark four-wheeled carts filled with all types of produce.

As on the Clyde, racing between rival vessels was never officially sanctioned but nevertheless frequently occurred. It is said that one San Francisco company issued a statement to all its captains that any of them caught racing would be fined five demerits, and anyone losing to the vessel of the rival concern would be fined ten!

Besides the regular ferry services, a number of excursions were provided with special trains bringing passengers to foster business. These were not always the comparatively quiet affairs that the owners would have wished. Over-indulged and exuberant passengers would sometimes vandalise train and ferry windows or participate in a fight or two.

The demise of the San Francisco ferries was hastened by the completion of the Golden Gate Bridge in May 1937. At first it was thought that only vehicular traffic would decline but, as elsewhere, the general ownership of the motor car meant that less and less foot passengers were carried, travellers preferring four wheels to two paddles.

The Sausalits commuters' run was abandoned in 1941 and the Oakland service terminated on the 10th February, 1957, being prematurely concluded by the breaking of the *Eureka*'s crankpin, thus ending the era of paddle propulsion across San Francisco Bay.

In Europe, one of the best-known passenger river services is still operated today by the Köln Dusseldorfer Rheindampfschiffahrt. The company is an amalgamation of two concerns which have operated paddle steamers from Cologne and Dusseldorf since 1826 and 1836 respectively. The modern Rhine fleet no longer consists of steam-driven paddlers but vessels which are either propelled by diesel-electric or Voith-Schneider machinery, enabling the age-old basic design of a paddler to be retained with its advantage of shallow draught, coupled with more economic operation.

One of the most popular tourist lakes in Europe is Lake Lucerne, twenty-three miles in length and with an average width of two miles. Against the magnificent backdrop of the Alps, the steamers of the Schiffahrtsgesellschaft Vierwaldstattersee (SGV) paddle their way on service from Lucerne, Fluelen or Alpnachstaad to one of the many smaller landing stages situated on the banks of the lake. A succession of paddle steamers has plied the lake since the iron paddle steamer *Stadt Luzern* under the command of Oberstlieutenant Franz von Elgger surprised, and perhaps even terrified, the crowds of spectators lining the shore in 1837.

It is to the European river and lake steamers that perhaps we should look to maintain and preserve the last company-owned paddle vessels operating a regular and useful service. Certainly their popularity is not in dispute during the tourist season and it would appear that the lake and river paddlers of Europe will continue to sail into the immediately foreseeable future.

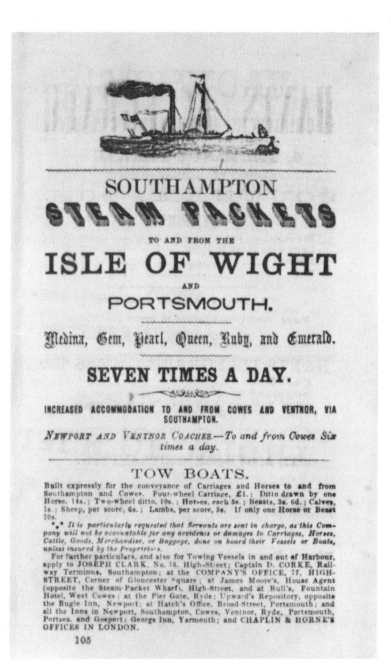

BANGOR CASTLE

Seen here at Belfast, the *Bangor Castle* was at that time owned by the Belfast, Bangor and Larne Steamboat Company.

In 1894 she left Northern Ireland for service with the newly formed Plymouth Excursion Steamship Company, owned by Captain Samuel Vincent, operating to Torquay and Falmouth. The *Bangor Castle* had been built in 1866 and Captain Vincent incurred considerable expense in maintaining the ageing vessel, with the result that the company failed and the ship was scrapped during the winter of 1899–1900.

GREENORE later CLOGHMORE

This small double-ended paddler of 217 gross tons was built by J. P. Rennoldson on the Tyne in 1896. She was originally named *Greenore*, a name she relinquished in 1912 to a much larger cross-channel steamer. Under both names she was employed by the London and North Western Railway on Carlingford Lough until 1921. At the beginning of the following year she was purchased by the Ribble Passenger Transport Company and received yet another change of title, becoming for six seasons the *Ribble Queen*. She was finally broken up in 1928.

This page taken from a mid-19th-century guide book advertises six of the paddle steamers which founded the services of the Southampton, Isle of Wight and South of England Royal Mail Steam Packet Company in 1861. Reference is made to the tow boats which the steamers towed behind them to and from the island for carriages and baggage.

'It is particularly requested that Servants are sent in charge, as this Company will not be accountable for any accidents or damages to Carriages, Horses, Cattle, Goods, Merchandise or Baggage . . .'

One can imagine the gesticulations from the 'Master' to his 'Coachman' being towed in the barge during a rough sea, some 20–30 yards astern of the steamer.

The steam launch built for Dr. Livingstone's exploration of the Zambezi River. Built by John Laird at Birkenhead, the vessel was 75 ft. long and made in three sections which could be assembled in the water. Her draught was 13 in.

Steam tug built for the Government for use in the shallow rivers of India. Constructed at Birkenhead by Laird, Sons and Co. she had a length of 220 ft., a beam of 38 ft. and a draught of 24 in.

A steel paddle steamer built by Alfred Yarrow during the second half of the 19th century for use on India's rivers. She had a length of 90 ft. and a draught of 15 in.

A Yarrow stern-wheeler photographed on the River Hooghly in India. Measuring
100 ft. by 24 ft., she had a draught of 13 in. and a speed of 13 knots. C. 1875

A paddle launch built by Alfred Yarrow for use on the rivers of Brazil. C. 1870

River boats at New Orleans in the 1850's.

Built in three sections this galvanised steel stern-wheel paddler was built by Yarrow & Co. for the United States of Columbia, in South America. She had a draught of only 10 in. with a length of 50 ft. and a beam of 10 ft.

VALIANT

The *Valiant* of 1902 was one of several river vessels constructed by J. White and Co. of the Isle of Wight for use on the rivers of Africa and South America.

This stern-wheeler was specially constructed by Yarrow for the Nile Expedition in only seventeen days. She had a length of 89 ft. and a beam of 18 ft. Her draught was a mere 18 in.

Another of the stern-wheelers constructed by Yarrows for the Nile Expedition in April 1885. She had a length of 138 ft. with a beam of 23 ft.

POTOMAC

The side-wheel paddler *Potomac* dated from 1880 when she was constructed by Charlan and Hollingsworth at Wilmington. In 1892 she was lengthened in order to accommodate the increased traffic on the Hudson River services on which she was employed until 1930, being then transferred to the Potomac River until withdrawn in 1948. Her three funnels situated athwart ships remained an unusual feature of her design and she is seen here nearing the end of her days on the 15th August, 1947, at Washington D.C.

HENDRICK HUDSON

This twin-funnelled side-wheel paddle steamer was one of a number operated on the Hudson River, New York, for commuters and excursions. Built in 1906 at the Marvel Shipyard, Newburg, the *Hendrick Hudson*, named after a director of the company which owned her, was of 2,847 gross tons with an overall length of 290 ft. 6 in. She was fitted with an inclined compound Fletcher engine capable of developing 6,200 horse power.

She is photographed here on the 10th July, 1948, during her final year of passenger service. For the following three years she awaited a new owner but no-one had a use for the old steamer and she was finally scrapped in 1951.

CITY OF NEW YORK

Pictured in New York Harbour in 1946, the *City of New York* had paddle boxes somewhat reminiscent of European vessels. She retained the tall funnel, which prevented a blowback of smoke onto her decks and passengers, which gave many of the American paddlers a somewhat antiquated appearance.

During the winter the vessels of the Keansburg Steamboat Company which were not required to maintain a reduced service, were laid up at Keyport, New Jersey, and the *City of New York* was unfortunately blown ashore and became a total loss during a hurricane in the early 1950's.

PRISCILLA

Originally named *Queen of the Sound*, the Fall River Line side-wheeler *Priscilla* was built in 1894 by a firm with the grand sounding title of The Delaware River Iron Ship Building and Engineering Company. She was one of the largest paddle vessels to operate on American coastal waters, being of 5,292 tons and powered by a massive set of compound engines. These engines developed 8,500 horse power and gave her a service speed of over 20 knots.

With a passenger capacity of 1,500 she operated on Long Island Sound for forty-three years and might have seen even longer service had not the Fall River Line ceased operations in 1937. *Priscilla* was towed to Baltimore during the following year and demolished.

COMMONWEALTH

The largest and last of the Fall River Line paddlers was the *Commonwealth* built at Philadelphia in 1908 by William Cramp and Sons. In general design she was a stretched version of other members of the fleet including the *Queen of the Sound* later *Priscilla*, already illustrated. 455 ft. 8 in. in length, her 11,000 horse power engines must rank as some of the most powerful ever to propel a paddle vessel, her machinery having a stroke of no less than 9 ft. 6 in. The *Commonwealth* never changed hands and was operated from 1908 until the shutdown of services in 1937, when she was towed to Baltimore for scrapping.

GREATER DETROIT

The *Greater Detroit* was built in 1925 for the 275 miles overnight run on Lake Erie from Buffalo, New York, to Detroit, Michigan, operated by the Detroit and Cleveland Steamboat Company. The vessel is perhaps better described as a liner than excursion or ferry steamship, for her cabins and staterooms were fitted out to provide the maximum comfort then available for her passengers. Her three funnels also provided her with the looks of a 'flyer'. After a quarter of a century of service the *Greater Detroit* was withdrawn in 1950 and after a period of inactivity was finally dismantled in the late 1950's.

PILGRIM

The Fall River Line side-wheeler *Pilgrim* built in 1882 had the distinction of being fitted with the largest simple beam engine ever fitted to a ship of this kind. She was withdrawn and scrapped in 1915 after a comparatively short life as a passenger steamer.

ROBERT FULTON

Another example of the Hudson River Day Line vessels was the *Robert Fulton* built in 1909 by the New York Shipbuilding Company at Camden, New Jersey. Of 2,168 gross tons, she was fitted with a vertical beam engine which had been originally fitted to the paddle steamer *New York* of 1887 and which had suffered a disastrous fire.

The *Robert Fulton* was employed on the Hudson River until 1955 and was 346 ft. in length overall being an enlarged and improved version of the *Potomac*. She is pictured at the mid-Hudson Bridge at Poughkeepsie, New York, in August 1938.

FRANCES

The beam-engine of the *Frances* is clearly shown in this shot of a typical American side-wheeler. Note also the lack of masts for passing under bridges and the precarious position of three crew members on top of her paddle box.

AVALON

One of America's best known stern-wheelers still in existence is the *Belle of Louisville* having previously sailed under the names of *Idlewild* and *Avalon*. As the latter she is seen here on 21st June, 1949, at East Liverpool, Ohio.

Unfortunately the name of this Canadian Pacific Railway stern-wheeler is not discernible. Similar in design to the American river paddlers, she at one time operated on Okanagan Lake in British Columbia.

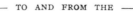

South Western & Brighton Railway Companies' Steam Packet Service

—— TO AND FROM THE ——

ISLE OF WIGHT

OCTOBER 1922, and until further notice

(Weather and other circumstances permitting).

S.S. "Duchess of Fife," "Duchess of Kent," "Duchess of Norfolk," "Duchess of Albany" and "Princess Margaret."

PORTSMOUTH HARBOUR AND SOUTHSEA CLARENCE PIER TO RYDE

	WEEK DAYS																SUNDAYS				
	a.m.	a.m.	a.m.	a.m.	a.m.	a.m.	p.m.	p.m.	p.m.	p.m.	p.m.	p.m.	p.m.	Thursdays only	p.m.	October only	a.m.	October only	p.m.	p.m.	p.m.	p.m
Portsmouth Harbour dep.	2.40	7.5	7.35	9.25	10.0	11.40	12.15	1.50	3.15	3.55	4.50	6.10	7.15		11.30		10.15		12.20	2.10	4.0	6.55
Southsea Clarence Pier ,,	..	..	..	..	10.10	11.50	..	2.0	..	4.5	5.0	..	7.25		..		10.25		12.30	2.20	4.10	7.5
Ryde Pier .. arr.	3.10	7.35	8.5	9.55	10.35	12.15	12.45	2.25	3.45	4.30	5.25	6.40	7.50		12.0		10.50		12.55	2.45	4.35	7.30

RYDE TO SOUTHSEA CLARENCE PIER AND PORTSMOUTH HARBOUR

	WEEK DAYS																SUNDAYS				
	a.m.	a.m.	a.m.	a.m.	a.m.	p.m.	p.m.	p.m.	p.m.	p.m.	p.m.	p.m.	p.m.	Thursdays only	Midt.	October only	a.m.	October only	p.m.	p.m.	p.m.	p.m
Ryde Pier .. dep.	6.45	7.55	8.40	10.10	11.10	12.55	2.20	3.5	4.0	4.50	5.45	6.50	9.25		12.5		11.10		1.10	3.10	5.0	9.25
Southsea Clarence Pier arr.	..	..	..	10.35	11.35	1.20	..	3.30	..	5.15	6.10	..	..		..		11.35		1.35	3.35	..	..
Portsmouth Harbour ,,	7.15	8.25	9.10	10.45	11.45	1.30	2.50	3.40	4.30	5.25	6.20	7.20	9.55		12.35		11.45		1.45	3.45	5.30	9.55

REVISED FARES :

	Single		Return	
	1st	2nd	1st	2nd
To Ryde Pier Gates, and vice versa. ...	2/2	1/7	4/-	3/2
	(Including all Pier Tolls)			
To Ryde Pier Head, and vice versa. ...	2/-	1/5	3/8	2/10
	(Exclusive of Ryde Pier Tolls)			

For particulars of

CHEAP DAY RETURN TICKETS

between Portsmouth Harbour, Southsea Clarence Pier and Ryde

SEE SEPARATE ANNOUNCEMENTS

ORDINARY RETURN TICKETS ARE AVAILABLE FOR TWO DAYS (Including day of issue and return).

Those issued on Saturday are available to return on the following Monday. Children between three and twelve are charged half-fares.

The connection between the Trains and Boats and *vice versa* is not guaranteed, neither will the Joint Companies be accountable for any loss, inconvenience, or injury arising from sea risks or delays.

Passengers are requested to look to their luggage on entering and leaving the Steam Packets, and before embarking to see it labelled to the Station or Pier where the journey of the owner terminates. Passengers are allowed to take with them, free of charge, the following amounts of personal luggage: 1st Class 150 lbs., 3rd Class 100 lbs. **Excess Luggage** will be charged for at the rates applicable.

Goods or Merchandise not allowed as passengers' luggage, and will be charged for at Parcels Tariff.

SEASON TICKET RATES :—First Class, Twelve Months, £9 : 0s. od. Six Months, £5 : 5s. od. Three Months, £3 : 0s. od. Two Months £2 : 9s 6d. One Month, £1 : 10s. od. Available for all advertised passages between Ryde, and the Piers at Portsmouth, exclusive of Pier Tolls.

Season Tickets, exclusive of Pier Tolls, are issued at half rates for residential purposes only, to all applicants under 16 years of age, and to Scholars, Students, Apprentices, Articled Clerks and Articled Pupils (in receipt of salary, wages, or any monetary allowance whatsoever, not exceeding 18/- per week), up to 18 years of age.

Quarterly Tickets may be extended to six or twelve months on payment of the difference between the periodical rates, but tickets must be promptly renewed or the privilege will be forfeited. Application for Season Tickets should be made at the Marine Superintendent's Office, Portsmouth Harbour Pier.

CONVEYANCE OF MOTOR VEHICLES (Which can be run on and off Boats with own power), Horses, Carriages Vans, Cattle, etc., TO & FROM THE ISLE OF WIGHT on Week Days, by powerful Steam Tug and Tow Boats.

(Weather and other circumstances permitting)

From PORTSMOUTH (Broad St. Slipway) for RYDE

About TWO HOURS before High Water.

From RYDE (George St. Slipway) for PORTSMOUTH

About HALF-AN-HOUR before High Water.

Information as to actual times of departure from Portsmouth and Ryde may be obtained at the Marine Superintendent's Offices, Broad Street, Portsmouth (Tel. 4655), Portsmouth Harbour Pier (Tel. 6077), or from the Station Master, Ryde (Tel. 247).

Senders or Owners of Horses, Carriages, Motor Cars, Live Stock, etc., by Tow Boat, take upon themselves all risk of Conveyance, and of loading or unloading, as the Companies will not be answerable for accidents or damage done to any property, live stock, etc. All traffic must be at the place of embarkation half-an-hour before time of sailing, and in charge of Senders' or Owners' Servants who must accompany it.

RATES (at Owner's Risk)

		£ s. d.
Motor Cars See Note (A)	not exceeding 10 cwt., Single Journey	1 1 0
	10 cwt., Return ,, (B)	1 16 0
	above 10 cwt., Single ,,	1 11 0
	10 cwt., Return ,, (B)	2 16 0
Motor Tricar	..	10 0
Motor Bicycle	..	3 0
,, ,, with Side Car	..	6 0
Bicycle	..	1 0
Hand Truck or Barrow	..	2 0
Hand Organ	..	2 8
Van, not exceeding 12ft. in length	(Loaded) £2 8 0	Empty 1 0 0

	£ s. d.
Van, not exceeding 15ft. in length	
(Loaded) £3 0 0 Empty	1 4 0
,, not exceeding 18ft. in length	
(Loaded) £4 0 0 .. ,,	1 10 0
Farm Waggon (Loaded) £2 0 0 ,,	16 0
Four-wheel Carriage	1 12 0
,, ,, ,, (Loaded)	2 2 0
Light 4-wheel Carriage, drawn by Ponies or 1 Horse	1 0 0
Gig, Cart or other 2-wheel Vehicle	16 0
Horse with Carriage	5 0
,, not with Carriage	7 0
Cattle, if under 10 in number .. each	£ 9

		£ s. d.
Cattle, if over 10 in number .. each		4 0
When only 1 Horse or Bullock in the Boat ...		10 0
Yearlings	.. each	3 0
Sheep, Lambs and Pigs—		
under half-a-score	.. each	1 0
over half-a-score up to 1 score		9 0
above a single score	per score	7 0
Calves	.. each	2 0
Servants, in charge, who must accompany all Horses, etc. each		1 0
Dogs	.. each	8
Hearse with Corpse	..	2 2 0

(A) Including Portsmouth Corporation Dues. (B) Return Tickets are available for one month. Motor Lorries, Steam Traction Engines, Circuses, etc., Quotations by special arrangements with Marine Superintendent.

BY ORDER.

In 1880 the London and South Western Railway and the London, Brighton and South Coast Railway formed an alliance to run the ferry link between Portsmouth and the Isle of Wight. This sailing bill of the 'Joint Fleet' of October 1922 shows the frequent service which was operated even after the summer rush of visitors had ceased. Note the reference to the carriage of motor cars which were transported in open barges towed by a tug independently of the passenger service.

REEDERIJ OP DE LEK

Owned by the Stoomboot Reederij op de Lek of Slikkervees in Holland, this three-decked paddler was a vessel capable of transporting passengers, goods or cattle. She was the 26th paddle steamer built by J. and K. Smit and delivered in 1911. The numeral 6 was added to her name in 1912. Throughout her life she ran twice daily between Schoonhoven and Rotterdam calling at no less than twelve landing stages on each single part of her journey.

In 1950 the *Reederij op de Lek 6* was sold out of service to Herr Karl Pfister of Ludwigshafen, seeing further use at that town as a floating restaurant. In 1976 she was purchased by two Hilversum musicians, Wijnand Key and Wim de Vriesl, and, after many difficulties, the old ship was towed back to Muiden in Holland and re-engined, refitted and restored by H. Schouter Ltd., re-entering service in 1977. She is now employed on cruises from Vreeswijk to Rotterdam and excursions in the neighbourhood of Amsterdam.

TRILLIUM

The Canadian side-wheel paddle ferry *Trillium* was constructed by the Polson Iron-works at Toronto in 1910 for service between Toronto and the offshore peninsula known as Toronto Islands. Following the Second World War, the popularity of the ferry service declined, and the *Trillium* together with another paddler named *Mayflower* were withdrawn. The latter was gutted for use as a soil barge and the *Trillium* narrowly avoided the same fate. The *Mayflower* proved unsuitable as a barge and consequently her sister ship remained intact although towed to a backwater and left to rot.

By the 1970's the Toronto Islands were enjoying renewed popularity and a feasibility study found that the old ferry could be returned to service at less cost than a new ship. She was reconditioned and renovated during 1974–5 by McNamara Marine of Whitby, Ontario, and by Herb Fraser and Associates of Humberstone and returned to her original service on the 19th May, 1976.

At present the double-ended vessel has a ferry capacity of 1,050 passengers and a certificate for 500 when used on excursions.

FRESHWATER

The *Freshwater* was built in 1927 at Cowes, Isle of Wight, by J. Samuel White and Co., for the Southern Railway ferry service between Lymington and Yarmouth, Isle of Wight, and occasional excursion work in the Solent. She replaced the paddler *Lymington*. Passing to the ownership of the British Transport Commission in 1948, she sailed on for a further eleven years, although mainly used as a relief vessel. Subsequent to the ordering of a new diesel car ferry which was to bear her name the suffix II was added to her title.

The *Freshwater* in her own way has contributed to the preservation of subsequent steamers in the British Isles, for it was on board this little paddler, during one of her final trips in September 1959, that Dr. Alan Robinson conceived the idea of forming a preservation society to encourage the retention of the remaining paddle steamers still in use at that time.

The subsequent history of the *Freshwater* after her service between the Isle of Wight and Lymington was more chequered. She was purchased by a Mr. Herbert Jennings and renamed *Sussex Queen*, but after an unsuccessful season in 1960, employed on short excursions along the Sussex coast, she was transferred to Bournemouth in the following year as a private venture to replace the Cosens-owned *Monarch*, which had been withdrawn and scrapped. Renamed *Swanage Queen* she was again unsuccessful with the result that she was offered for sale in October 1961. By this time necessary repairs would have been costly and the ship was sold and towed to Belgium for breaking in May 1962.

ORWELL

The Great Eastern Railway Company owned the *Orwell* built in 1873 for general service including excursions on the river after which she was named. Although similar in appearance to a tug of the period, she was not in fact used for towing duties. The *Orwell* lasted about twenty years before being dismantled in the 1890's.

LYMINGTON

The first steel paddle steamer for the London and South Western Railway Company service to Yarmouth in the Isle of Wight was launched by Day, Summer and Co. of Southampton on the 6th April, 1893. During the summer she was also engaged in peak season excursions to some of the Island's piers. An unusual feature was the lack of a bridge, the Captain and Helmsman being situated on a tiny platform in front of her funnel. As the ship had to be turned around in the narrow confines of the river adjacent to the railway pier, extreme accuracy of width had to be estimated by her Masters.

The *Lymington* was employed throughout the year and withdrawn from railway service in 1929.

KILLINGHOLME

One of the most unattractive paddle steamers ever to be employed on excursions was the *Killingholme*, one of two similar steamers built in 1912 for the Grand Central Railway and intended as ferries between New Holland and Hull. In fact both 'ugly ducklings' undertook this service for twenty-three years until superseded by more modern replacements in 1934. The *Killingholme* was retained as a standby vessel and was used during the summer for excursion work on the River Humber. She was finally broken up in July 1945.

DELTA QUEEN

Very few places in the world have ever been able to offer trips of more than two or three days' duration, apart from the mighty paddlers of the Mississippi, which because of their size could offer adequate sleeping accommodation. These two advertisements, dated 1954 and 1955, are for the Greene Line *Delta Queen*, both suggesting 20-day cruises on board.

HANSA

The German-owned *Hansa* started life in 1905 as one of a fleet of thirty vessels ordered by the London County Council in 1905 for a continuous bus-stop type of service along the Thames, her original name being *King Alfred*. This ambitious scheme was opened by the Prince of Wales on board this vessel on the 17th June, 1905, between Hammersmith and Greenwich, but the ships operated at a loss with the result that when the L.C.C. called an end to the service on the 15th December, 1907, the total deficiency for two and a half years' working was £162,499. Fourteen of the vessels were retained for further service on the river by a private company and the rest were sold far and wide.

The *King Alfred* which had a capacity of 530 passengers had been built by the Thames Iron Works at a cost of £6,000. She was sold in May 1909 for £1,050 to O. May of Memel for service on the Rhine and named *Memel*. In the early 1920's she went to Hamburg under the name of *Hansa* where she served the Hamburg-Cuxhaven route. She was later employed on the Hamburg-Blankenese Sunday service. Surviving the war, *Hansa* was withdrawn and scrapped during the winter of 1964-5.

KAISER WILHELM

The *Kaiser Wilhelm* is still fitted with her original twin cylinder compound diagonal engines of 168 H.P. fitted by Dresdener Machinenfabrik in 1900.

KAISER WILHELM

The *Kaiser Wilhelm* is now Germany's oldest operational paddle steamer. Built in 1900 at Dresden for the Oberweser Dampfschiffahrt Gesellschaft she operated on the River Weser from Hamelin. When withdrawn in 1970, she was acquired by the Lauenburger Elbe Shipping Museum near Hamburg, and is now happily maintained in an operational condition. She is used on a varied programme of weekend charters and public sailings from May to October of each year.

ELAN

Typical of many of the smaller European river ferries which ran up to about 1914 were these French vessels of about 100 tons which provided a service from Rouen to La Bouille.

WILHELMINA

This Dutch paddle steamer of 1891 was built for the Nederlandsche Stoomboot Reederij of Rotterdam for service along the Rhine. For the first five years of her life she had a much longer name sailing under the somewhat awesome title of *Wilhelmina Prinses Der Nederlanden*. Constructed of iron by the well-known Dutch shipyard of L. Smit at Kinderdijk, *Wilhelmina* was reconstructed in 1935 receiving more sheltered accommodation aft of her funnel.

When the German Forces occupied Holland in 1940 she was renamed *Willem II*, as Dutch ships bearing the name of living members of the Royal House were no longer allowed. On the 17th October, 1944, she was destroyed by bombing at Cologne. Although raised later, this 223-ton vessel was not worthy of repair and was accordingly scrapped.

VATERLAND

The Rhine excursion steamer *Vaterland* is seen approaching a typical river landing stage at Der Ehrenbreitstein, Coblenz. Note the partially retracted mainmast for passing beneath some of the Rhine bridges. The *Vaterland* was constructed in 1926 by Sachsenberg of Cologne and although sunk at Neuwied on the 19th March, 1945, was raised and returned to service in 1949. Although withdrawn from passenger service in 1973 the *Vaterland* of 490 tons is still in existence, being laid up at Neihler Harbour, North Cologne.

DIESSEN

The *Diessen* provides a service on the Ammersee in West Germany and retains the looks of a mid-19th-century lake steamer although she was constructed as late as 1908 by J. A. Maffei of Munich. After more than sixty years as a coal-fired steamer the *Diessen* was re-engined during 1974–5 and is now diesel powered. A similar vessel, the *Andecks* (1907–55), is still in existence on the lake and in use as a houseboat.

DARTMOUTH CASTLE

With her almost cartoon-like funnel, the *Dartmouth Castle*, operated by the River Dart Steamboat Company between Dartmouth and Totnes, sets the scene for a typical summer excursion at the beginning of the century.

CAPTAIN STURT

Although the majority of Australia's Murray River paddlers were side-wheelers, there were also a number of larger stern-wheelers employed on wider sections of the river. Such was the *Captain Sturt* now converted to a houseboat at Goolwa. Note the typical hogged appearance of her hull.

COONAWARRA

Still paddling along the Lower Murray River is the diesel powered paddler *Coona-warra* of 255 gross tons. She is equipped with 16 cabins and total accommodation for 42 passengers offering Australians a week-long holiday on board. Largely wooden built she originally carried wood up and down the river to fuel the once numerous passenger-carrying paddlers.

Her weekly itinerary is to leave Murray Bridge every Monday during the summer and to arrive at the township of Morgan on Wednesdays, before commencing her return journey downstream, to arrive back at Murray Bridge about 4 p.m. on Fridays. Surveyed annually by the Commonwealth Department of Shipping and Transport the *Coonawarra* is operated by the South Australian Government Tourist Board.

AIOCA and COONAWARRA

At one time the *Aioca* was consort to the *Connawarra* and both vessels are seen here at Murray Bridge landing stage, a few miles before the river enters Lake Alexandrina, South Australia.

GALLIA

Built at Zurich in 1913, the *Gallia* is generally acknowledged to be one of the fastest of the Swiss Lake steamers. She has fortunately retained her traditional appearance complete with scrolls on her bows. She normally undertakes a daily sailing to Fluelen on Lake Lucerne.

PATRIA

The Italian lake steamer *Patria* was built at Genoa in 1926 and originally named *Savoia*. She is of 286 gross tons and has a capacity of 900. During 1945 she was damaged by air attack and returned to service with a more modern ecliptical funnel. She is still steam powered but was converted to oil fuel in 1953. For the past few years she has been used only as a relief vessel during the peak of the summer season.

MILANO

With her quaint stovepipe funnel and awning, the Italian-owned lake steamer *Milano* is set against the picturesque background of Lake Como.

QUEEN ELIZABETH

One of the larger river steamers to ply on the River Thames was the *Queen Elizabeth* constructed in 1895 by Edwards and Company of Millwall for a Mr. Edward Shand. Of 141 gross tons she was licensed to carry no less than 709 passengers and it is to be hoped that for the comfort of those who sailed on her that this number was not often reached. She was advertised to leave London Bridge daily except on Fridays for Kew, Richmond and Hampton Court.

About 1897 her ownership was transferred to the rather grand sounding 'Queens' of the River Steam Ship Company and in 1913 she was sold to Mr. J. T. Mears of Richmond for continued Thames service. The war no doubt put paid to his plans and the *Queen Elizabeth* was scrapped shortly after the close of the war.

MAID OF THE LOCH

The last major British paddle steamer to be built was announced in 1951 but did not enter service until two years later. Ordered by the British Transport Commission from A. & J. Inglis of Glasgow, the *Maid* is equipped with oil-fired engines and is capable of some 15 knots. She operates a summer service from Ballock to Ardbui on Loch Lomond.

Of somewhat traditional design the *Maid of the Loch* has an unusual feature in that her superstructure is entirely of aluminium thus reducing her weight and draught, a necessary precaution for the shallower parts of the Loch. It would appear that apart from preserved vessels the *Maid* is destined to become the last operational paddle steamer in Great Britain employed on pleasure cruises.

TRITON

The former Royal Navy paddle steamer *Triton* built in 1882 was not finally scrapped until 1962, although she had been out of active commission for very many years. The *Triton* was originally a naval survey ship and as such she undertook a number of long assignments to the Pacific in the 1880's and 1890's. When decommissioned, her engines were removed and scrapped, and she was converted to a training ship for the Gravesend Sea School, anchored off Gravesend. Later she was moved to the West India Dock in London and used as an accommodation ship, before finally being advertised for disposal in 1961. Some months later she was towed to Holland for demolition by Jacques Bakker and Zonen of Zelgate.

TRITON

The old survey ship lays in West India Dock shortly before her final voyage to the breakers.

HJEJLEN

The second oldest paddle steamer still in service is the Danish vessel *Hjejlen* completed in June 1861. She also holds the distinction of being the world's smallest operational paddler with a gross tonnage of only 39.

Constructed by Baumgarten and Burmeister of Copenhagen, her only salt water voyage was the first stage of a difficult journey from her makers to the Silkeborge Lake where she has spent the whole of her long life. Sailing under her own steam from Copenhagen to Randers she then travelled up the River Gudenaaen. From Bjerring Molle she was towed by eight horses and six men. At Frisholt Skov she was lightened by removing all disposable gear which reduced her draught by 5 in. When she eventually arrived at Silkeborg a further difficulty had to be overcome as the ship had to be transported across a road in order to reach the waters of the lake. This obstacle was overcome by enlisting the aid of rollers and a large number of workers from a near-by paper mill.

The *Hjejlen* has been patronised by Royalty, His Majesty King Frederik VII attending her maiden voyage in 1861 and on the occasion of her centenary His Majesty King Frederik IX was present. She presently operates from June to August and has become a major tourist attraction in this part of Denmark.

MAINZ

Similar in general looks to the *Rudesheim* is the *Mainz*, the last paddle steamer to be constructed for passenger service on the Rhine. Built in 1929 by Christof Ruthof at Mainz, her original passenger capacity was 2,680 on a tonnage of 586, but this has now been reduced to 1,720 to provide better facilities for those on board. It was the *Mainz*, luckily free of major war damage, which re-opened the Cologne to Mainz direct service on the 14th April, 1949.

She is pictured here before the addition of painted paddle vents and it is left to the reader to decide between the décors of *Rudesheim* and *Mainz* as to which presents the most aesthetic appeal.

EINHEIT

The oldest paddle steamer afloat in East Germany is the *Einheit* constructed at Blasewitz in 1873. Powered by a steam compound engine of 200 H.P. and paddle wheels constructed of spruce she was until 1925 the largest passenger ship operating on the River Elbe. In 1926 she received a new wheel house and steering gear.

Surviving the war the veteran vessel was given a complete overhaul in 1950 and equipped with an upper deck, some six years later she was split into two halves and lengthened by over 9 ft., a saloon was fitted and new and lighter wheels installed. Since her maiden voyage the *Einheit* has theoretically steamed thirty-seven times around the Equator.

In 1975 the vessel was in static use as a restaurant at Pillnitz. During her long career she has served under three names being originally launched as the *Germania*, then taking the title of *Lössnitz* in 1928 and receiving her current name in 1950. In her final form she is 180 ft. in length.

RUDESHEIM

The powerful Rhine paddle steamer *Rudesheim* of 536 tons was built in 1926 at Cologne as the *Rheinland*. On the 12th March, 1945, she was sunk at Kaiserwerth and after extensive work re-entered service in 1951.

In 1965 she was renamed to allow her original title to be bestowed on a new motor vessel. The *Rudesheim* is seen here in 1977 showing the rather incongruous paddle vents painted on all paddlers of the Koln-Dusseldorfer Line during that year.

DRESDEN

The river port of Dresden provides a fine setting for the paddler of the same name. This vessel was the first post-1914–18 war steamer to be placed in service and in design was more advanced than any other vessels then serving on the Elbe. In order to assist river navigation she is fitted with twin rudders and possessed covered accommodation from the start.

In June 1946 she suffered a disastrous fire and was re-fitted during the following year. The *Dresden* remains a useful member of the VEB Fahrgastschiffahrt, a state-controlled company known as the Weisse Flotte (White Fleet).

6 The Paddle Steamer at War

The first major use of paddle steamers in war occurred during the American War of Independence. When President Lincoln, on the 19th April, 1861, declared a blockade of the ports of the seceding states, it was not long before the blockade became effective, threatening the export of cotton on which the Southern States relied.

Intending blockade runners were ensured of a quick and valuable profit should their efforts be successful. Consequently approaches were made to shipowners, particularly on the Clyde, for fast paddle steamers capable of running the gauntlet of the blockading forces. In order not to involve the sellers in any form of political scandal, the destination and trade for which the blockade runners were intended were seldom disclosed and, instead, purchases were made for the 'South American trade', 'a Spanish firm' or even 'the Emperor of China'.

Ships were often purchased on the stocks, two examples being the *Roc* and the *Fox* which in 1862 were being constructed for the Belfast trade, replacement vessels being laid down immediately they were launched, to the delight of their builders. The ships themselves were stripped of interior fittings and painted grey as a form of camouflage. Smokeless fuel was in demand and on occasions the crews were dressed in inconspicuous clothing.

An example of the profit made is exemplified by the *Diamond* which had been intended for use by J. Henderson & Son of Renfrew. Although purchased second-hand for £4,000, before she had been placed on station, her owners accepted the 'Emperor of China's' offer of £7,500.

As far as Britain was concerned, the Admiralty were slow in realising the potential of steam and, in fact, few major warships have ever been propelled by paddle wheels. To be fair, there were many difficulties in applying this form of propulsion to ships of the line, not the least being the vulnerability of wheels and engines to damage by gunfire.

Once the paddle steamship had been established as a reliable form of transport, navies throughout the world adopted and adapted paddle steamers for a multitude of tasks. Paddle frigates, survey ships and tugs abounded towards the end of the 19th century and during the 1914–18 war many ex-pleasure steamers were adapted as minesweepers, and patrol and examination vessels. In fact a class of paddle minesweepers was built for the British Navy and thirty-two vessels of this class were delivered between January, 1916, and March, 1918. It is said that these were built as a direct result of the success of ex-pleasure steamers impressed in sweeping coastal waters, the design being generally based on the British Channel excursion steamer *Glen Usk*, the shallow draught of the paddle steamer being ideal for mine clearance. Five further paddlers were ordered in 1918 but cancelled following the Armistice.

During the Second World War many excursion steamers were again impressed into Admiralty service and formed into six mine-sweeping flotillas. Their other duties included service as auxiliary anti-aircraft vessels, many being stationed on the River Thames to protect the approach to London. Many paddle steamers took part in the rescue of the British and Allied troops from Dunkirk, several being lost in the process.

As naval tugs, paddle steamers have performed sterling service. Dockyard paddle tugs were stationed at every major dockyard in Britain and at many posts of the British Empire. In fact, as late as 1956–7 a class of diesel-electric paddle steamers was ordered and delivered, all of which are still in service with the British Navy.

A further use for the paddle steamers was as gunships and river patrol vessels in China and throughout the Far East. Similar occupations for paddle vessels were found by many other navies where manoeuvrability, draught and size were of paramount importance.

The first paddle steamers for the British Navy were the *Comet*, launched at Deptford in 1822, and the *Monkey*, constructed a year earlier as a private venture. They were mainly employed as tugs or dispatch boats. In 1827 Captain Sir John Ross proposed a polar expedition using a steam-propelled paddle vessel; his idea was turned down but undaunted he undertook such a venture privately and sailed on the *Victory* from Woolwich on the 23rd May, 1829.

In the 1830's both Sir James Graham, the First Lord of the Admiralty, and Sir Thomas Masterman Hardy, famous for his connection with the death of Nelson and who had become First Sea Lord, favoured steam propulsion. In 1831 a despatch vessel, *H.M.S. Black Eagle*, was commissioned and armed with an eighteen-pounder gun. The first true paddle warship for the British Navy was *H.M.S. Gorgon* of one thousand one hundred and eleven tons which carried two ten-inch and four thirty-pounder guns and was launched in 1837. Three years later she took part in the bombardment of Acre under the command of Admiral Stopford.

During the 1830's and 40's the Admiralty took delivery of a number of sloops and frigates, the largest of which was *H.M.S. Terrible* of some one thousand four hundred tons.

WALTON BELLE

The *Walton Belle* of 1897, after service as a minesweeper in the Royal Navy during the 1914–18 war, was fitted out for further government service as a hospital ship in 1919 under the uninspiring name of *H.C.3*. As such she was intended for use in the Russian campaign on the Dvina to transport wounded to larger ships to convey them home. She was finally released in May 1920 and once again resumed excursions.

The photograph shows the *Walton Belle* as a minesweeper. Note the gun mounted on her fore deck.

Following a number of experiments in 1843 between a screw and a paddle vessel of similar size, which resulted in the screw sloop *H.M.S. Rattler* showing superiority over the paddler *H.M.S. Alecto*, the British Navy adopted screw propulsion but the existing paddle steamers continued to serve until replaced towards the end of the century.

The 20th-century use of paddle steamers in defence not only includes the sterling work undertaken by minesweepers and tugs but also duties as fleet messengers, troop transports, anti-aircraft ships, contraband control examination vessels and hospital ships. During the 1914–18 war two Thames River excursion paddlers found themselves fitted out in the latter rôle and sailed as far as the White Sea, covering a distance of some two thousand miles and averaging over a hundred miles a day whilst making their epic journey.

Admiral Sir Reginald Bacon in his book titled *The Dover Patrol* mentions the work of British paddle minesweepers in the flotilla of miscellaneous ships that were based at Dover during the 1914–18 war.

'The paddle minesweepers were the safest vessels for sweeping owing to their small draught and to their great speed—some ten to eleven knots—which enabled the moorings of the German mines to be immediately cut. These then floated to the surface and did not remain entangled in the sweep, and were therefore less dangerous to the sweeping vessel. The only defect of the paddle minesweepers was their inability to keep at sea or to sweep efficiently in bad weather.

'The principal factor in safe minesweeping is the shallow draught of the vessels employed. Trawlers drawing 15 feet suffered many losses while on patrol, when mines were laid, and when searching and sweeping dangerous areas. Paddle minesweepers drawing 8 to 9 feet 6 inches as a maximum were at least 75% safer than trawlers...

'... The paddle minesweepers were commanded by Lieutenants Royal Naval Reserve and Royal Naval Volunteer Reserve who had obtained mates' certificates. The remainder of the officers were Lieutenants and Sub-Lieutenants, Royal Naval Volunteer Reserve. The crews were composed of volunteers taken from all professions and a large proportion of the deck-hands had never been to sea before...

'... The standard of work done by the paddlers was high and though they were continually stopped by bad weather they never failed in an attempt to leave harbour at daylight and make a good effort to carry out the work which they had been ordered to do.'

PRINCE OF WALES

The *Prince of Wales* as *H.M.S. Prince Edward* laying anti-submarine nets off Condia in the Mediterranean during the 1914–18 war.

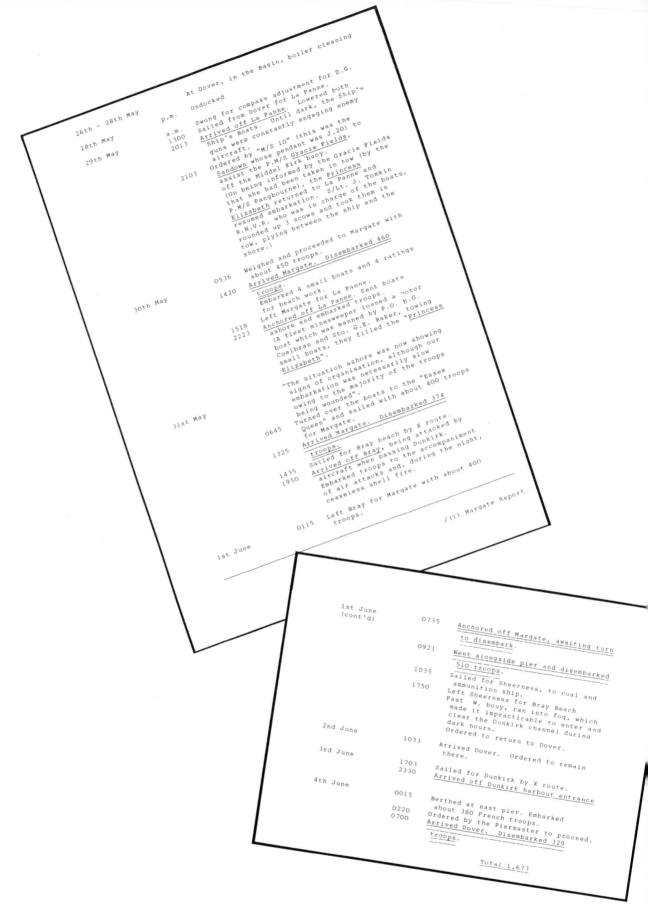

Date	Time	Entry
26th - 28th May		At Dover, in the Basin, boiler cleaning
28th May	p.m.	Undocked Swung for compass adjustment for D.G.
29th May	a.m. 1300	Sailed from Dover for La Panne. Arrived off La Panne. Lowered both Ship's Boats. Until dark, the Ship's
	2013	guns were constantly engaging enemy aircraft. Ordered by "M/S 10" (this was the _Sandown_ whose pendant was J.20) to assist the P.M/S _Gracie Fields_,
	2103	off the Middel Kirk buoy. (On being informed by the Gracie Fields that she had been taken in tow (by the P.M/S _Pangbourne_), the _Princess Elizabeth_ returned to La Panne and resumed embarkation. S/Lt. J. Tomkin R.N.V.R. who was in charge of the boats, rounded up 3 scows and took them in tow, plying between the ship and the shore.)
30th May	0536	Weighed and proceeded to Margate with about 450 troops.
	1420	_Arrived Margate. Disembarked 460 troops._ Embarked 4 small boats and 4 ratings for beach work.
	1518 2223	Left Margate for La Panne. Sent boats _Anchored off La Panne._ Sent boats ashore and embarked troops. (A fleet minesweeper loaned a motor boat which was manned by P.O. H.G. Coalbran and Sto. G.E. Baker, towing small boats, they filled the "Princess Elizabeth".
31st May		"The situation ashore was now showing signs of organisation, although our embarkation was necessarily slow owing to the majority of the troops being wounded". Turned over the boats to the "Essex Queen" and sailed with about 400 troops for Margate.
	0645	_Arrived Margate. Disembarked 374 troops._
	1325	Sailed for Bray beach by X route.
	1435 1950	_Arrived off Bray_, being attacked by aircraft when passing Dunkirk. Embarked troops to the accompaniment of air attacks and, during the night, ceaseless shell fire.
1st June	0115	Left Bray for Margate with about 400 troops.

/(1) Margate Report.

Date	Time	Entry
1st June (cont'd)	0735	_Anchored off Margate, awaiting turn to disembark._
	0921	_Went alongside pier and disembarked 510 troops._
	1035	Sailed for Sheerness, to coal and ammunition ship.
	1750	Left Sheerness for Bray Beach Past W. bouy, ran into fog, which made it impracticable to enter and clear the Dunkirk channel during dark hours. Ordered to return to Dover.
2nd June	1033	Arrived Dover. Ordered to remain there.
3rd June	1703 2330	Sailed for Dunkirk by X route. _Arrived off Dunkirk harbour entrance_
4th June	0015	Berthed at east pier. Embarked about 380 French troops.
	0220 0700	Ordered by the Piermaster to proceed. _Arrived Dover. Disembarked 329 troops._

Total 1,673

An excerpt from the log of the paddle minesweeper _Princess Elizabeth_ during the Dunkirk evacuation.

During the Second World War, a number of excursion paddle steamers were fitted with anti-aircraft guns and, together with several other vessels similarly converted, defended the sea and river approaches to London from hostile attack. These units became affectionately known as 'Eagle' ships in the Royal Navy, named after the *Royal Eagle*, the prototype in this rôle.

When an armada of little ships sailed to rescue the British Expeditionary Force from Dunkirk in June, 1940, no less than five ex-excursion paddlers were sunk in the process. Nevertheless many successful return trips were made by paddle steamers with their decks crowded with three or four times their normal certificated capacity. Such was their success that when the *Medway Queen* was withdrawn in 1963, the Dunkirk Veterans' Association attempted to preserve the vessel as a memorial to the evacuation.

DUNKIRK

In 1940, a well-known commentator of the British Broadcasting Corporation, J. B. Priestley, produced a wartime booklet in aid of the British Red Cross, the main part of which comprised a transcript of a broadcast made by him immediately after the evacuation of troops from Dunkirk. The work of impressed paddle steamers is vividly described under Mr. Priestley's chapter heading *Excursion to Hell*.

'But here at Dunkirk is another English epic. And to my mind what was characteristically English about it—so typical of us, so absurd and yet so grand and gallant that you hardly know whether to laugh or cry when you read about them—was the part played in the difficult and dangerous embarkation not by the warships, magnificent though they were, but by the little pleasure steamers. We have known them and laughed at them, these fussy little steamers, all our lives. We have called them "the shilling sicks". We have watched them load and unload their crowds of holiday passengers —the gents full of high spirits and bottled beer, the ladies eating pork pies, the children sticky with peppermint rock. Sometimes they only went as far as the next seaside resort. But the boldest of them might manage a Channel crossing to let everybody have a glimpse of Boulogne. They were usually paddle steamers, making a great deal more fuss with all their churning than they made speed; and they weren't proud, for they let you see their works going round. They liked to call themselves "Queens" and "Belles"; and even if they were new there was always something old-fashioned, a Dickens touch, a mid-Victorian air, about them. They seemed to belong to the same ridiculous holiday world as pierrots and piers, sand castles, ham and egg teas, palmists, automatic machines and crowded, sweating promenades. But they were called out of that world—and, let it be noted, they were called out in good time and good order.

Yes, these *Brighton Belles* and *Brighton Queens* left that innocent foolish world of theirs to sail into the inferno, to defy bombs, shells, magnetic mines, torpedoes, machine-gun fire—to rescue our soldiers. Some of them, alas, will never return. Among those paddle steamers that will never return was one that I knew well, for it was the pride of our ferry service to the Isle of Wight—none other than the good ship *Gracie Fields*. I tell you, we were proud of the *Gracie Fields*, for she was the glittering queen of our local line, and instead of taking an hour over her voyage used to do it, churning like mad, in forty-five minutes. And now never again will we board her at Cowes and go down into her dining saloon for a fine breakfast of bacon and eggs. She has paddled and churned away—for ever. But now—look—this little steamer, like all her brave and battered sisters, is immortal. She'll go sailing proudly down the years in the epic of Dunkirk. And yet our great-grandchildren, when they learn how we began this war by snatching glory out of defeat, and then swept on to victory, may also learn how the little holiday steamers made an excursion to hell and came back glorious.'

Almost certainly the last paddle-propelled tugs for the British Navy were delivered in 1956-7. A class of seven vessels was ordered with engines powered by four diesel generators, connected in series coupled to two independent propulsion motors, each capable of eight hundred nautical horse power.

The Navy ordered these vessels expressly for moving aircraft carriers and other large vessels in confined waters. Besides harbour towing duties, each ship is equipped for salvage and with three-quarters of their hull length occupied by their diesel-electric engines, they give an impression of tremendous power.

GRACIE FIELDS

The paddle steamer mentioned so nostalgically by J. B. Priestley was launched by the radio and film star whose name she bore from the yard of Thornycrofts at Southampton on the 8th April, 1936. She was intended for all-year service between Southampton and Cowes, Isle of Wight, and excursion work, to supplement the other paddlers of the Southampton, Isle of Wight and South of England Royal Mail Steam Packet Company, better known at that time as Red Funnel Steamers. She was the last British paddle vessel to be fitted with a graceful counter stern.

Of 393 gross tons and capable of 14 knots, *Gracie Fields* became a popular member of the fleet although her general design was somewhat dated being based on that of the *Princess Elizabeth* of 1927, which in turn was generally similar to that of the company's *Princess Mary*, dating back to 1911.

During her first year of service she sailed from Southampton to Brighton to give a cruise to children from an orphanage at Peacehaven of which Miss Gracie Fields was patron. An incident of more serious note occurred on the 15th July, 1939, when a Royal Air Force flying boat from Calshot collided with the vessel at the entrance to Southampton Water. The starboard wing of the flying boat was shattered and the machine fell into the sea but the crew escaped injury. The port bow of Gracie Fields was damaged and her foremast snapped, pieces of metal from the flying boat were showered on her passengers but fortunately no-one was hurt.

Impressed into service with the British Navy she was based at Dover and on the 28th May, 1940, sailed to Dunkirk bringing back 281 troops. The next day she returned and with 750 more soldiers on board she was attacked by German aircraft and hit amidship. Although attempts were made to tow the stricken vessel back to England, she sank before reaching safety at 1.30 a.m. on the following morning.

GRACIE FIELDS

Seen here off Cowes in 1936 with an open bridge, she was subsequently fitted with an enclosed wheelhouse.

PRINCE OF WALES

The ex-Isle of Man steamer *Prince of Wales* serving as *H.M.S. Prince Edward* lies at moorings in Valetta Harbour at Malta during the 1914–18 war.

STURDY

The Dockyard Service tug *Sturdy* launched on the 12 November, 1912, by Thornycroft was one of a once numerous class of paddle tug employed by the British Navy in almost every naval port. She was of 690 tons displacement and capable of 12 knots. Towards the end of her career she was renamed *Swarthy* and scrapped at Passage West in March 1961.

CHELTENHAM

Taking a rest from her minesweeping duties the Racecourse Class *H.M.S. Chelten-ham* lies at Zeebrugge shortly after the end of the 1914–18 war.

EPSOM

Looking every inch a warship, although designed merely for minesweeping, the *Epsom* awaits commissioning. She was an example of the Racecourse Class of paddle sweepers ordered by the British Admiralty during the First World War.

Built by George Brown and Company of Greenock and launched on the 4th May, 1916, she survived the war and was sold in March 1922 for breaking at Inverheithing.

LORNA DOONE

This fine study of the ex-Admiralty minesweeper *Atherstone*, later *Queen of Kent*, shows her in Southampton Water on the 18th May, 1949, after she had been purchased by Red Funnel Steamers of Southampton. With a gross tonnage of 798 and a speed of 16 knots she was a costly vessel to maintain. She was renamed *Lorna Doone* after a previous unit of the same fleet which was not reconditioned after war service. After only four seasons with the company she was sold for breaking and towed to Dover on the 13th March, 1953.

GRINDER

One of the class of seven paddle-driven diesel electric paddle tugs built between 1956 and 1958, *Grinder*, built by William Simons of Renfrew, had a crew of 5 officers and 15 ratings. Each of her wooden feathering floats are made of Canadian rock elm and are 12 ft. 6 in. in length. Most of *Grinder*'s service has been at Portsmouth naval base.

7 The Wheel at Work

The first idea of towing a ship by paddle propulsion seems to have come from Jonathan Hulls, an Englishman who registered a patent in 1736 'for moving a boat by a steam engine or for the application of an atmospheric engine to actuate or propel a boat by paddles for towing vessels in and out of harbours, etc'. The basic idea was for an outrigged paddle wheel at the stern of the tow-boat, worked by a pulley system from the engine situated in the hull of the vessel. The tow-line to be attached to the stern of the vessel. Mr. Hulls does not appear to have persevered with the idea, which must have had considerable stability problems and it was to be many years before towing by steam became a practical possibility.

The commencement of towing duties for paddle-propelled vessels was almost synonymous with the general introduction of steam propulsion. The *Charlotte Dundas*, which can truly be called the first successful British steamboat, in 1802 promptly began towing duties, proving her worth on the Forth and Clyde Canal by hauling two laden sloops a distance of nearly twenty miles in six hours.

Sixteen years later in 1818, *The Tyne Steamboat*, the first steamer to carry passengers in English waters between Newcastle and the mouth of the River Tyne, was found employment on towing duties. By 1821 there were no less than fourteen paddle tugs on the Tyne alone, the progenitors of hundreds of like vessels employed not only in British coastal waters but also throughout the world.

For the remainder of the 19th century the paddle tug, holding its own against the screw and paddle steam tugs, undertook a multitude of duties. The decline of the paddle tug began after the turn of the century when the increased efficiency of the screw, coupled with economic factors, precluded the building of further tonnage. Subsequent to the First World War very few new vessels were ordered, the last major paddle tug programme being run in the 1950's by the British Admiralty with the seven diesel-electric tugs already mentioned in the preceding chapter. Many of the early steam paddle tugs continued in service until the 1950's and 60's until, like the excursion steamers, one by one they sailed, worn out by their exertions, to the breakers.

In Europe, from the middle of the 19th century, the number and capability of the River Rhine paddle tugs increased apace, several trade wars breaking out between rival companies. In the early days it was not unknown for stones and other objects to be thrown at passing ships, the majority fortunately falling short of their targets. By the turn of the century large paddle tugs, often pulling or pushing barges, provided a substantial and frequent service along the entire course of the Rhine.

After the First World War many side and stern-wheelers were transferred from the Elbe to meet the ever-increasing demand, many of these being scuttled or sunk by bombing during the second conflict. In May, 1945, only three paddlers remained afloat, with fifty-five sunk along the hundred and seventy-kilometre stretch of river from Mannheim to Köblenz.

By the end of that year several had been refloated and the survivors continued in service until the 1950's, when, one by one, they went to the breakers. By 1969, only the *Raab Karcher XV Oscar Huber* remained but sadly even this last remaining example of a once numerous fleet was not considered worthy of preservation.

The first recorded use of a paddle vessel used for trawling in the British Isles occurred in 1863, when a small paddle vessel was seen off Dunbar, but she was evidently unsuccessful for no further reports appeared about her. In 1870, F. Rushworth of Grimsby ordered a paddle trawler but it was not until the end of that decade, when a recession in towage occurred along the north-east coast, that a number of tugs were converted for trawling. These conversions were often thought up and executed by crew members. On the 2nd November, 1877, the paddle tug *Messenger* set out for her first catch, and it would appear that she met with some success. Her fish realised £7.10s.0d. (£7.50) and in addition she earned £5 for towing a sailing ship into South Shields during the same voyage. In the 70's and 80's several rugged paddle trawlers were constructed, among them the *Tyne* which operated from Scarborough.

Besides the more obvious duties of towing ships into and out of ports throughout the world, many other uses have been made of paddle-driven vessels. Certainly the development of river settlements could not have been achieved so speedily without the communication afforded by the early steamers. The fertile banks of the Mississippi, the land of the Louisiana sugar kings and the rich cotton plantations of America's South owe much to the tall funnelled steamboats. They enabled the planters and growers to transport their products to outlets which grew into great international trading posts. In Australia, the lumber boats manoeuvred massive floats of timber hundreds of miles along the navigable inland rivers, opening up new trade routes and bringing wealth to the lumberjack.

We must not forget the part that paddlers have played as salvage vessels, often venturing into mountainous seas to cast a line aboard a sailing vessel being driven into danger. Paddle trawlers cast their nets and oyster dredgers scoured their catch from the murky bottom up to the outbreak of the First World War, whilst other more ornate paddlers, often excursion vessels, have tendered trans-oceanic liners with passengers and baggage.

The paddle steamer as a work-ship has also gleaned its moment of glory in the guise of Royal Yachts, it being said that Queen Victoria preferred the smooth passage of such vessels to any other form of marine transport. Indeed she travelled in no other type of Royal vessel, the screw-driven Victoria and Albert being accepted after her death.

And so the list to which the feathered wheel has been put goes on—train ferry—showboat—paddle chain ferry—hospital ship. No-one can say that the use of the paddle steamer has not been inventive or resourceful.

CARRIER

Looking every inch a workboat the *Carrier* was constructed in 1858 by Scotts' yard at Greenock being a direct descendant of the *Leviathan* of 1849, the first train ferry in the world. Both vessels were constructed for the Edinburgh, Perth and Dundee Railway Company for their Tay River service.

After some time at Granton, the *Carrier* was sold in 1884 to the Isle of Wight Marine Transit Company, and operated between Langston on the mainland and Bembridge. The service was unsuccessful and after being laid up for some years the 243 gross tons vessel was sold to Sweden for further service in 1892.

TRIUMPH

The 1867 iron-built tug *Triumph* of Scarborough was converted for trawling and is seen here in that guise. She was sold to Londonderry in 1882 and reconverted for towing duties.

TRIUMPH

Another view of the paddle trawler *Triumph* together with four other vessels of similar type in harbour.

TOM REES NO. 2

The *Tom Rees No. 2* was built at Pittsburgh, U.S.A., in 1869 at the yard of Thomas Rees and Sons. She was a typical Ohio River tow boat and it was as such that she was employed on the river until a fatal day in February 1910.

The wooden-hulled stern-wheeler had tied up near Cluster Islands before attempting to navigate further up the reaches of the river. On the night of 9th February there was sufficient water and under the command of Captain Abraham Gould she maintained a good head of steam and set sail shortly after daybreak on the following day. Unfortunately the wooden hull of the forty-one-year-old steamer buckled and she sank near Mahan's Light without loss of life.

The *Tom Rees No. 2*'s machinery, hull and superstructure were salvaged and scrapped, but some of the heavier relics remained at the bottom of the river for over fifty years, when a whistle, numerous pipe fittings and pieces of ornamentation were scooped from the river bottom by a dredger seeking to deepen the river bed in 1962.

CONQUEROR

Several British tugs were designed with their funnels athwartship and the *Conqueror* of 1884 when scrapped in 1956 was the last remaining vessel with this feature.

During her seventy-two years of service she undertook duties at London, Middlesbrough, Dundee, Leith and the Tyne and even included a period under the French flag at Boulogne when she was given the French title of *Conquerant*. She is seen here in the Tyne on the 6th August, 1938.

CONQUEROR

It was not often that passengers were given the opportunity of crossing the Channel by tug, even in Victorian and Edwardian times, but the *Conqueror*, owned by the Elliot Steam Tug Company of London, provided such an opportunity, for in the summer she was fitted out as an excursion steamer. Built in 1897 and of only 141 gross tons, besides her forays to France, she was notable for being the first vessel to run from London to Dover on a regular basis and it was from the latter port that she probably undertook this excursion to Boulogne sometime before 1914. *Conqueror* continued in her dual capacity until withdrawn in 1925. The vessel had no connection with the previous twin-funnelled *Conqueror*.

SOME INCIDENTS IN THE LIFE OF THE
LORD ELGIN

During her long service on cargo work for her Southampton owners the *Lord Elgin* carried many unusual loads ranging from elephants to hairpins, but perhaps one of the more out of the way requests was for a packet of bird seed. The request coming from the Trinity House lightship at Calshot Spit. Apparently a parrot had fallen from a liner passing the lightship and the bird had been picked up by the Trinity House crew and rescued. Having no food for their pet a packet of parrot seed was essential and in due course the *Lord Elgin* came alongside with the required sustenance.

On another occasion a cow which should have embarked on the vessel decided that ship life was not suitable and promptly jumped into the water endeavouring to swim to freedom. Captain Diaper, then mate of the *Elgin*, eventually rounded up the animal by chasing it in a small launch, the *Island Enterprise*, and lassoing the cow around her horns before bringing her back to the landing stage.

Livestock were a regular part of the *Elgin*'s cargo both to and from the Island and amongst the most difficult to get aboard were pigs. Some merriment was caused amongst onlookers at Cowes Pontoon one day when several of the ship's officers were seen trying to catch hold of runaway pigs. They would endeavour to get behind the pigs and to jump onto their backs in order to catch hold of their ears and tails to bring them to justice. Altogether the scene must have resembled a wild west rodeo.

When the *Lord Elgin* was scrapped in 1955, Captain Joe Sewley had achieved thirty years in command of the vessel and had amassed no less than 8,607 trips totalling 223,790 miles between the Isle of Wight and the mainland. He stands here in front of the old steamer during one of her final trips at Cowes.

LORD ELGIN

This 203 gross tons vessel had the distinction of becoming the last British cargo paddle steamer. She was broken up in 1955. Besides being a cargo vessel the *Lord Elgin* had a long and distinguished career on passenger service.

She was constructed in 1876 for the Galloway Steam Packet Company of Leith, passing to the South coast in 1881 for passenger service from Bournemouth. In 1909 the Southampton, Isle of Wight and South of England Royal Mail Steam Packet Company took her over from her Bournemouth owners together with their other assets and vessels.

Between the wars and up to her demise the *Lord Elgin*, stripped of her once ornate saloons and fittings, plodded between Southampton and the Isle of Wight, taking all types of cargo from pins to elephants to the Isle of Wight, including cars and lorries. Her regular run was to leave Southampton at 11.30 a.m. and return at 2.30 p.m. at a steady 8 knots. The *Lord Elgin* steamed away from the Royal Pier on the 13th May, 1955, to near-by Northam where she was broken up by Messrs. Pollock and Brown.

GELBSTERN

This unusual vessel is the German oyster catcher *Gelbstern* of 1910 bringing up six plentiful baskets from the sea bed.

FRENCHMAN

An example of a dual-purpose paddle steamer was the *Frenchman*, which for many years was employed as a tug and excursion vessel. Originally constructed and named *Coquet* in 1892 at North Shields, she was operated by the towing firm of T. Gray and Company. Renamed *Frenchman* she was rebuilt in 1906 and served as a pleasure steamer at Bridlington during the summer season.

In the early 20's when Gray's and a number of other towing companies amalgamated to become the United Towing Company, she continued in this double existence until superseded by a screw vessel in 1928. For very many years her hull was used as a coal-bunker at Kingston-upon-Hull, being finally disposed of in the 1960's.

BRILLIANT STAR

The sea-going tug *Brilliant Star* approaches a berth at Bristol around the turn of the century. She was one of the largest tugs to paddle up the River Avon and her design is reminiscent of many of the Rhine tugs of the same period.

SUPPAN

The Austrian, German and Dutch tugs of the Danube and Rhine rivers were similar in design. The *Suppan* was one of five sister ships built between 1921 and 1927 for service on the Danube from Passau to the Danube Delta. When withdrawn in 1966 she had served forty-five years in the purpose for which she was built at Schiffs-werft, Budapest.

KONINGIN WILHELMINA

This typical example of a Rhine paddle tug was originally Dutch-owned and built by
Gebr. Sachsenberg of Rosslau, making her maiden voyage in August 1926. Two years
later she was transferred to the Vereinigungsgesellschaft Rheinischer Braunkohle-
bergwerke Company of Cologne and renamed *Gustav Wegge*.

Together with a number of other tugs under the same ownership she was always
beautifully maintained. In 1945, in order to avoid capture by the advancing allied
forces, the *Koningin Wilhelmina* was scuttled by her crew. During the following year
she was salvaged and repaired entering a new lease of life on the Rhine until 1957,
when she was laid up. Her end was not far away however and in 1959 this giant of the
river was sold for breaking.

HER MAJESTY

A Hampshire-based paddle steamer of the Southampton, Isle of Wight and South of England Royal Mail Steam Packet Company, *Her Majesty* was constructed by Barclay Curle and Company in 1885. After a long life as a ferry between Southampton and Cowes with occasional use in her early days as an excursion vessel, she was withdrawn in 1927 and converted to a car ferry between the mainland and the Isle of Wight. With her aft saloon removed she could carry up to 12 cars and a not insignicant amount of deck cargo.

In addition the elderly paddle steamer was used for tendering liners anchored in Cowes Roads, in particular the French transatlantic liner *Normandie*. Passengers disembarking from the pride of the French fleet must have found a stark contrast inside the 19th-century paddler but fortunately their journey was a short one.

Her Majesty was retained at Southampton after the outbreak of the Second World War and sunk by a German bomb in 1940. Upon being subsequently raised she was found unfit for further use and broken up.

ELIE

Withdrawn after fifty years of continuous service as a tug. The *Elie* was built in 1912 for the Great Western Railway Company and named *Pen Cur* for service at Fishguard. She was unusual in having two single diagonal engines instead of the more common side-lever type. In 1927 she was sold to the Tees Towing Company and renamed *Ingleby Cross*, five years later passing to her final owners the Grangemouth and Forth Towing Company. Under the name of *Elie* she was based at Methil although sometimes was seen as far afield as Rosyth.

After being withdrawn and scrapped in 1962 she was replaced by yet another elderly paddle tug, the *Roher* of 1905. The latter only had a short working life at Methil being broken up in 1966.

BOURNEMOUTH QUEEN

Besides tendering the international passenger liners which regularly called at Southampton, paddle steamers of the Southampton fleet were often employed carrying passengers to warships of the British Navy which opened their decks to visits. Such an occasion is pictured here, with a load of passengers having the doubtful choice of embarking onto *H.M.S. Shropshire* either by steeply sloping gangway or by the swaying platform operated by a crane.

The *Bournemouth Queen* made this trip to Spithead on the 16th May, 1937, when *H.M.S. Shropshire* was on station for the King George VI Coronation Review.

OSBORNE

Launched in 1874, the Royal Yacht *Osborne* was mainly used by the Prince of Wales for royal visits to the Mediterranean, Spain and Portugal. In 1884, shrouded in black, she carried the body of Prince Leopold, son of Queen Victoria, from Cannes to England, and, when the Queen died in January 1901, *Osborne* was among the vessels which escorted her remains from Osborne House in the Isle of Wight to the mainland. She remained on royal service until 1906 when replaced by a new screw-driven steam yacht which took her name.

175

UNITED SERVICE

The full meaning of a dual-purpose vessel is clearly illustrated in these two photographs of the tug and excursion vessel *United Service* which operated for many years along the North coast of Britain.

In the first print she is shown towing the brigantine *Anna* into Great Yarmouth in 1888 in the midst of a severe gale, whilst the second photograph depicts her crowded with trippers out for a 'trip round the bay' some forty years later.

WEXFORD and *SEABURN*

Two typical examples of general duties tugs on the North East coast were the Sunderland-based *Wexford* and *Seaburn* which are seen awaiting their next task on the 16th August, 1939.

8 Paddle Steamer Oddities

Any new invention always brings its quota of freaks and oddities and the paddle steamer was no exception. The possible advantage of twin hulls was realised as early as 1814, when the world's first steam warship, named *Demologos*, was built at New York to a design prepared by Robert Fulton. Her hulls were fifteen feet apart with a single sixteen-foot diameter paddle wheel in the centre. One hull contained the engines and the other the boilers and the *Demologos* was armed with twenty thirty-two-pounders. The ship never saw action, however, and was destroyed by an explosion on the 4th June, 1829. A similar arrangement was tried out on the Thames in 1850 in a vessel named *Gemini*, which again proved unsuitable, the area between the hulls becoming clogged with water thrown up by the revolving paddles.

A number of oddities were designed to make the passage across the English Channel more comfortable, amongst them the *Castalia*, another vessel built on the principle of the catamaran. The distance between hulls was twenty-six feet with two wheels in tandem. Although acknowledged as a comfortable ship, clogging was still apparent and she never reached her design speed.

In 1875, Sir Henry Bessemer devised a ship with a swinging saloon pivoted between two hulls, the idea being that the passengers would be maintained in equilibrium during a rough sea. Two pairs of paddle wheels were fitted in an attempt to give a service speed of twenty knots. Named *Bessemer*, she sailed for Calais on a relatively calm sea, but it soon became apparent that the paddler was slow to answer the helm, and she had considerable trouble in trying to enter Calais harbour. At the third attempt there was a violent collision with the pier. The ship was arrested until a bill for £25,000 for damages was agreed. On the return journey the *Bessemer* also collided with Dover pier, her maiden trip being perhaps the most costly enterprise ever undertaken by a paddle vessel. On returning from her second voyage, during which there had been faults with the swinging saloon, the *Bessemer* again came into contact with Dover pier, after which Sir Henry, very much the poorer but no doubt much wiser, withdrew the strange craft.

Another oddity was the *London Engineer* of 1818, constructed at Rotherhithe for a service to Margate. Twin paddle wheels fitted internally were assisted by air forced into the waterway. Again, the design was unsuccessful and the *London Engineer* was soon withdrawn.

The largest and grandest paddle steamer of the 19th century, the *Great Eastern*, can also be truthfully described as an oddity, even her launching which was undertaken broadside to the water being an innovation in 1858. Although a failure as a passenger vessel, it is to her credit that she laid the first commercially successful transatlantic cable from Europe to America in 1866.

The conversion of warships to pleasure steamers can also be described as unique. Such a fate befell *H.M.S. Melton* and *H.M.S. Atherstone*, both ex-paddle minesweepers constructed in 1916. Purchased by the New Medway Steam Packet Company they became, in 1927, *Queen of Thanet* and *Queen of Kent* respectively, being employed on excursions from Chatham, Southend and Margate, including cross-channel day trips to Calais and Boulogne. Later both vessels were sold for service from Southampton, in 1949 becoming the *Solent Queen* and *Lorna Doone* before being withdrawn and scrapped in 1951 and 1952 respectively.

This sleek river paddle steamer built by Alfred Yarrow at his yard at the Isle of Dogs had a draught of only 6 in. With a length of 45 ft. she had a speed of 8 miles an hour.

Double-ended vessels were built to provide a quick turn-round, especially on ferry services, including three similar ships for the railway connection between Portsmouth and the Isle of Wight in the 1880's.

To find a paddle steamer serving in the United States Army is also an oddity but the mighty stern-wheelers *General Newton* and *Mississippi* have both served the U.S. Corps of Engineers as river inspection vessels.

Strangely, there are few recorded examples of paddle steamers in service as private yachts, unless one includes examples of paddle-driven, privately-owned river boats such as the tiny *Guildford Belle*, which have been converted to this form of propulsion by enthusiastic engineer owners.

Nevertheless, we must not decry these freaks and oddities, for each in its own way has added to the store of knowledge which others have been able to draw upon in maintaining and operating more successful types of paddle craft.

DUCHESS OF EDINBURGH

The double-ended hull of the *Duchess of Edinburgh* is clearly seen in this photograph taken whilst under maintenance at Newhaven. She was one of three similar vessels built for the railway connection between Portsmouth and the Isle of Wight. Another peculiarity was the placing of her two funnels athwartship.

The *Duchess of Edinburgh* was constructed in 1884, the 342 gross tons vessel remaining in service throughout the year until replaced and scrapped in 1910.

STUDLAND BELLE

Wooden sea-going clinker-built paddle steamers were a rarity at the end of the 19th century and therefore it must have come as a surprise when the fast-growing seaside resort of Bournemouth first saw the diminutive *Studland Belle* in 1912. She had been built some eight years earlier and named *Advance* for service at Dundee and was purchased by her Master, Captain S. Shippick, for service from Boscombe and Bournemouth Piers to Studland Beach, a beauty spot at the foot of the Purbeck Hills. The *Studland Belle* had the distinction of being the first Sabbath breaker in this part of the South coast, when on the 3rd August, 1913, she made an excursion from Poole to Swanage.

After only two seasons she caught fire due to a stove being left unattended, and for many years her hull lay forlornly on the site of the present Poole Power Station, indeed it is said that the 'bones' of the 72 gross tons paddler were incorporated in the foundations of the power station.

LE STANLEY

Built by Alfred Yarrow for L'Association Internationale du Congo for use of the explorer Stanley on the River Congo and its tributaries. She was built in portable sections for transport overland.

TALISMAN

It is perhaps a little unfair to call a diesel electrical-powered paddle steamer an oddity, but the *Talisman* dating from 1935 was certainly the odd one out as far as Clyde excursion vessels were concerned. Built by A. and J. Inglis whose yard had produced many steam-powered paddlers, the *Talisman* ran her trials in June 1935 and recorded a speed of 17½ knots on four oil engines coupled to direct current diesel generators which in turn powered a double armature motor on the paddle shaft. What was even more creditable however was the fact that 14 knots could be attained on only two engines.

Entering service for the London and North Eastern Railway Company's service from Craigendoran, her engines did not prove entirely satisfactory and several breakdowns occurred. Nevertheless *Talisman* was requisitioned for service by the Admiralty on the 24th June, 1940, and converted immediately to an anti-aircraft vessel and renamed *H.M.S. Aristocrat*. A more important task befell the vessel in 1944 when she was chosen and fitted out as a headquarters ship for the Mulberry Harbour at Arromanches. On D-Day she was involved in a collision and put into Portsmouth for repairs, returning to the French coast when they had been completed. In 1945 *H.M.S. Aristocrat* sailed into the Scheldt after the liberation of Antwerp.

When she returned to the Clyde in 1946, under her original title she was given an extensive refit and resumed her services from Craigendoran until 1953 when she was re-engined. Reappearing in May 1954 the *Talisman* took up service on the Wemyss Bay-Millport-Kilchattan Bay route. Since 1948 the vessel had been operated by the British Transport Commission and latterly under the control of the Caledonian Steam Packet Company who decided after the 1966 season that the *Talisman* should be withdrawn. In October 1967 the thirty-two-year-old paddler was towed to Dalmuir and broken up by Arnott, Young and Company.

LUCY ASHTON

The last 19th-century paddle steamer in the Clyde to remain in service was the *Lucy Ashton*, a diminutive ship of only 271 tons. Built in 1888 for the British Steam Packet Company and capable of carrying 903 passengers she retained the old-fashioned feature of having her bridge aloft of her single funnel for the whole of her life. *Lucy Ashton* was originally fitted with a single diagonal engine but this was replaced in 1902 by compound machinery after a serious mechanical failure.

This Clyde veteran was based at Craigendoran and initially employed on the Holy Loch service, later she was transferred to the Garelochead route on which she served the greater part of her life. She remained on passenger service throughout both world wars and was finally withdrawn in February 1949 being towed to Faslane for breaking up. However her story did not end there, because in the following year she was acquired by the British Shipbuilders Research Association for experimental purposes. Stripped of her steam engines and paddle wheels, jet engines were attached to her hull and *Lucy Ashton* became the first jet-engined ship in the world. She was finally dismantled in 1951.

This 1926 sailing bill from Rothesay by the Royal Mail steamer *Columba* is headed
'The Royal Route' because the vessel transversed part of a journey undertaken by Queen Victoria a generation previously.

THE ROYAL ROUTE

1926

CHEAP DAY EXCURSIONS
FROM
ROTHESAY
TO
KYLES OF BUTE,
TARBERT AND ARDRISHAIG
By R.M.S. "COLUMBA"
(OR OTHER STEAMER),

APRIL TILL SEPTEMBER.

GOING			RETURNING		
Rothesay, leave	10-15	a.m.	Ardrishaig, leave	1-0	p.m
Colintraive, ,,	10-40	.,	Tarbert,	1-40	,,
Tighnabruaich, ,.	10-55	,,	Tighnabruaich, ,,	2-40	,,
Tarbert, ,,	11-55	,,	Colintraive, ,,	2-55	,,
Ardrishaig, arrive	12-40	p.m.	Rothesay, arrive	3-30	,,

RETURN FARES:

To COLINTRAIVE or TIGHNABRUAICH (valid day of issue only),
Cabin, 2/3.   Fore-Cabin, 1/6.

To TARBERT or ARDRISHAIG (valid day of issue only, or Friday or
Saturday till Monday).   Cabin, 5/-.   Fore-Cabin, 3/6.

Tickets can only be had at MacBrayne's Office, Rothesay, or on Board Steamer.
1926.   DAVID MACBRAYNE, LTD., 119 Hope Street, Glasgow.

THE BUTEMAN, LIMITED, ROTHESAY

GUILDFORD BELLE

This delightful little paddler and river boat will never feature in the history of any
major steamer company but has brought many hours of delight to her engineer
owner.

LIBA LIBA 6

Yet another use of a diesel engine to propel a paddler is shown in the *Liba Liba 6* of Renmark, South Australia. A number of these ungainly vessels are available for holiday use in cruising the tributaries and courses of the Murray. Each is of extremely shallow draught to avoid snagging on fallen trees which abound in and on the sides of the waterways.

LIBA LIBA

Another of the holiday *Liba* boats paddles her way past the outskirts of Renwick, South Australia.

MISSISSIPPI

A vessel of unusual history and use was the stern-wheeler *Mississippi* operated by the United States Army Engineer District of Memphis for the Mississippi River Commission and withdrawn from service on the 19th April, 1961. She plied the muddy waters of the river for thirty-three years, serving as a tow-boat when flood control and navigational improvements were being made and operating twice-yearly inspection trips of the lower Mississippi by the River Commission, the shallow draught being extremely useful during periods of low water.

Constructed on the Ohio River in 1927, she received a cabin which had been made five years previously in New Orleans for the steamer *Leota*, a dredge-tender originally built in 1899 and which on rebuild in 1922 had also been named *Mississippi* but which had been declared unserviceable in 1926.

Her design was modelled along the lines of a typical stern-wheel packet boat of a century previously. During her working life she plied 1,000 miles of the lower River Mississippi below the town of Cairo and 200 miles of the upper river. She was also to be seen over a hundred miles up the Missouri and Ohio Rivers, all of the Atchafalaya River and the length of the canal from Morgan City to New Orleans.

When withdrawn the paddle steamer *Mississippi* gave her name to a specially constructed twin-screw propeller of adjustable pitch.

9 The Decline of the Paddler

It is generally acknowledged that the decline of the paddle steamer cannot be attributed to any particular cause. It was brought about by a combination of circumstances, both social and economic.

If any one cause is to be singled out for the decline, as far as the excursion steamer was concerned, it can be put down to the more sophisticated forms of entertainment and travel that became available in the 1920's and 30's. In theory, with more people taking longer holidays, the paddlers should have done well, but holiday-makers began to prefer the covered entertainment provided by Winter Gardens, Theatres and Cinemas to the wind-lashed decks of ageing paddle steamers.

Undoubtedly, the char-à-banc and later saloon coaches took their share of passengers, largely at the expense of the marine excursions. The first signs of decline were the withdrawal of some long day outings shortly after the First World War, operators preferring to concentrate on shorter hauls. This was perhaps self-destructive in that the variety of excursions was immediately affected.

When the family car became popular and within the reach of many middle-income families, during the 30's, the writing was indeed on the wall. During the 1939 season some of the larger excursion steamers such as Campbell's *Devonia* were laid up, the paddle steamer operators awaiting the final outcome of the European political scene, before making any final decisions regarding further use.

After the war, conditions were a little better, the retention of petrol rationing coming to the operators' aid. By this time, however, the remaining excursion paddle steamers were well past their prime. Even between the wars few companies had ordered new tonnage, preferring to repair rather than replace.

Now came further factors which affected the popularity of the ships. The rising cost of coal and oil, of which some vessels devoured enormous quantities, had to be taken into consideration. The British Board of Trade, ever seeking increased standards of safety in all ships, issued regulations specifying new types of lifebelts, for example, which involved no little expense. These factors affected not only British excursion vessels; declining paddle fleets were apparent all over the world for much the same reasons.

In the 1950's and 60's the decline increased momentum. The cost of replacement by more modern vessels had risen so high as to make replacement of any ship—paddle or screw—that was to earn its keep only during the summer months an impossibility. Thus was the end of these little ships which for over one hundred years had been an intrinsic part of the seaside scene.

The few paddle steamers that were left in the 1970's began to be subject to active preservation in either a static or operational rôle, as we shall read in the next chapter.

CLACTON BELLE

'The Beginning and The End'. In 1890 the *Clacton Belle* was launched as the proto-type of the Thames Belle steamers by Denny's of Dumbarton followed by three similar vessels during the following six years. In the top photograph the *Clacton Belle* is seen on trials. Note her telescopic funnel designed especially for London's bridges.

After a lifetime of excursion service she was withdrawn in 1929 and the second photograph shows the veteran steamer in the process of demolition by Messrs. T. W. Ward at Grays, Essex. The deckhouse aft of her funnel was added a few years after being placed in service.

The first attempt to re-open paddle steamer excursions from the South Devon resort of Torquay after the war was in 1946 when the South Western Steam Navigation Company purchased the elderly *Essex Queen* which had started life as the *Walton Belle* in 1897 and seen service on the Thames. Renamed *Pride of Devon* she operated the 1947 and 1948 seasons only and was then laid up at Southampton, being broken up three years later in 1951.

P. & A. CAMPBELL LTD. & BRITISH RAILWAYS

THROUGH STEAMER AND RAIL BOOKINGS
From Cardiff and Penarth via Ilfracombe
To the Undermentioned Stations in

DEVON & CORNWALL

Commencing on June 1st, and continuing until September 23rd, 1950.

AUGUST, 1950.

TIMES OF SAILINGS AS FOLLOWS :

Leave CARDIFF

AUGUST		AUGUST	
Tues. 1	12.15 p.m.	Thur. 17	9.45 a.m.
Wed. 2	‡9.0 a.m.	Fri. 18	11.50 a.m.
Thur. 3	9.0 a.m.	Sat. 19	9.45 a.m.
Fri. 4	12 noon.	Sun. 20	9.15 a.m.
Sat. 5	†9.45 a.m. 12.30 p.m.	Mon. 21	†9.30 a.m.
Sun. 6	9.0 a.m.	Tues. 22	†9.45 a.m.
Mon. 7	9.15 a.m.	Wed. 23	11.30 a.m.
Tues. 8	†10.15 a.m. 3.5 p.m.	Thur. 24	†7.30 a.m.
Wed. 9	12 noon.	Fri. 25	9.0 a.m.
Thur. 10	†8.15 a.m.	Sat. 26	9.45 a.m.
Fri. 11	9.20 a.m.	Sun. 27	9.30 a.m.
Sat. 12	9.30 a.m.	Mon. 28	9.45 a.m.
Sun. 13	9.30, 10.45 a.m.	Tues. 29	11.50 a.m.
Mon. 14	9.15 a.m.	Wed. 30	9.45 a.m.
Tues. 15	11.15 a.m.	Thur. 31	9.15 a.m.
Wed. 16	9.35 a.m.		

Leave ILFRACOMBE

AUGUST		AUGUST	
Tues. 1	5.0 p.m.	Thur. 17	6.15 p.m.
Wed. 2	‡6.15 p.m.	Fri. 18	5.45 p.m.
Thur. 3	6.15 p.m.	Sat. 19	6.0 p.m.
Fri. 4	5.45 p.m.	Sun. 20	6.45 p.m.
Sat. 5	†5.15, 5.30 p.m.	Mon. 21	†6.15 p.m.
Sun. 6	7.0 p.m.	Tues. 22	†7.0 p.m.
Mon. 7	7.0 p.m.	Wed. 23	9.0 p.m.
Tues. 8	†7.15, 7.45 p.m.	Thur 24	12.45 p.m.
Wed. 9	9.0 p.m.	Fri. 25	6.0 p.m.
Thur. 10	†4.0 p.m.	Sat. 26	6.0 p.m.
Fri. 11	2.0 p.m.	Sun. 27	6.0 p.m.
Sat. 12	6.0 p.m.	Mon. 28	5.45 p.m.
Sun. 13	3.45, 6.0 p.m.	Tues. 29	4.45 p.m.
Mon. 14	6.0 p.m.	Wed. 30	5.45 p.m.
Tues. 15	5.0 p.m.	Thur. 31	6.45 p.m.
Wed. 16	6.0 p.m.		

† Via Weston-super-Mare. ‡ Via Porthcawl.

Ordinary Bookings to ILFRACOMBE on the above dates.
For Sailing Times, Fares, etc., see Special Bills and Daily Papers.

THROUGH FARES.

From CARDIFF to	First Class Rail and Saloon on Steamer		Third Class Rail and Saloon on Steamer	
	Single	Monthly Return	Single	Monthly Return
	s. d.	s. d.	s. d.	s. d.
Barnstaple (Jct. and Town)	14 0	22 3	12 0	20 2
Bideford	17 2	25 9	13 11	22 6
Braunton	12 1	19 11	10 11	18 7
Bude	32 1	44 2	22 10	34 9
Chapelton	15 7	24 6	13 2	21 8
Copplestone	22 11	33 0	17 5	27 4
Crediton	25 2	35 8	18 10	29 1
Devonport	39 3	52 8	27 3	40 5
Eggesford	20 3	30 0	15 10	25 4
Exeter (St. David's and Central)	27 3	37 11	20 0	30 7
Exmouth	31 0	42 11	22 2	33 11
Fremington	15 1	23 5	12 7	20 11
Holsworthy	28 6	39 11	20 9	31 11
Instow	16 4	25 2	13 6	22 1
Lapford	21 8	31 3	16 7	26 2
Launceston	30 7	42 2	22 1	33 5
Morchard Road	22 4	32 6	17 0	27 0

THROUGH FARES.

From CARDIFF to	First Class Rail and Saloon on Steamer		Third Class Rail and Saloon on Steamer	
	Single	Monthly Return	Single	Monthly Return
	s. d.	s. d.	s. d.	s. d.
Newton St. Cyres	25 11	36 9	19 2	29 10
Okehampton	28 5	39 11	20 8	31 11
Ottery St. Mary	32 6	44 8	23 1	35 1
Padstow	42 9	56 11	29 5	43 3
Paignton	36 9	49 6	25 8	38 4
Plymouth (North Rd. & Friary)	39 3	52 8	27 3	40 5
Portsmouth Arms	17 9	27 0	14 4	23 4
Seaton	36 5	49 0	25 5	38 0
Sidmouth Junction	31 7	43 6	22 7	34 4
South Molton Road	18 11	28 3	14 11	24 2
Tavistock	33 11	46 8	24 1	36 5
Torquay	36 0	49 0	25 3	38 0
Torrington	18 11	28 3	14 11	24 2
Umberleigh	16 6	25 2	13 4	22 1
Wadebridge	40 11	54 5	28 1	41 7
Wrafton	12 4	20 2	11 1	18 9
Yeoford	23 9	34 5	17 11	28 3

The Fares do not include Pier Tolls at Ilfracombe (3d. each way).

Passengers on arrival at Ilfracombe proceed from the Pier to the Station, and vice versa, at their own expense. Passengers can proceed from Ilfracombe by any train after the arrival of the Steamer at Ilfracombe. For times of trains see the British Railways Time Tables

AVAILABILITY OF TICKETS.—Ordinary Single Tickets. Three days, i.e., the date shown on the Ticket or the first or second day following such date (Sunday is not counted except when the Ticket is dated for that day).

Monthly Return Tickets. Return Halves of Tickets available for one calendar month, but not after September 23rd or such later date as the steamer service may be in operation. The journey may be broken at any station on line of route covered by the Tickets held.

Children under Three Years of Age, Free ; over Three and under Fourteen Years of Age, Half-Fare.

150lbs. of Luggage allowed each First Class Adult Passenger, and 100lbs. each Third Class Passenger.

Similar Bookings are also in operation to Cardiff from the Stations named. See Bills issued by the British Railways.

NOTICE.—The Company will not hold themselves responsible for the safety of any Passengers or intending Passenger before embarking on or after disembarking from any of their Steamers ; reserve to themselves the right of calling at any ports or places for any purposes whatsoever, and do not hold themselves responsible to sail at the advertised times of departure or guarantee punctuality of arrival of Steamers, but will use every endeavour to carry out the sailings as announced.

The issuing of Through Tickets is subject to the Conditions and Regulations referred to in the Time Tables, Books, Bills and Notices of the Steamboat Company, The Railway Executive and Proprietors on whose Steamboats, Railways, Coaches or Piers they are available ; and the holder by accepting a Through Ticket agrees that the respective Undertakings and Proprietors are not liable for any loss, damage, injury, delay or detention caused or arising off their respective Steamboats, Railways, Coaches or Piers. The contract and liability of each Undertaking and Proprietor are limited to their own Steamboats, Railways, Coaches or Piers

TICKETS TO BE OBTAINED ON BOARD STEAMERS.

For further particulars, etc., apply to

P. & A. CAMPBELL Ltd., Pier Head, Cardiff.

P. & A. CAMPBELL Ltd., 10, Quay, Ilfracombe ; or

P. & A. CAMPBELL Ltd., Cumberland Basin, Bristol.

This sailing bill issued in 1950 was an attempt to popularise the Cardiff-Penarth-Ilfracombe service operated by P. and A. Campbell Ltd. by means of offering combined tickets with British Railways to many towns and resorts in South Devon and Cornwall.

EMPRESS

The paddler with a printed obituary. Such was the esteem in which the Cosens paddle steamer *Empress* was held by her owners that the company took the trouble of pointing out to the public the trip on which she was engaged during her last week of service from Weymouth during September 1955.

She was fitted with the last set of oscillating engines on the South coast which have been preserved and are on permanent exhibition at Southampton's Maritime Museum.

ROYAL EAGLE

The *Royal Eagle* once the pride of the London River steamers is here seen being dismantled in 1953, after being laid up at Whitewall Creek on the River Medway for three years. She was a victim of rising costs and lack of patronage, a fate which befell many paddle steamers in the 50's and 60's.

SHOWBOAT EMBASSY

In the 1950's when it became clear that passenger receipts from seaside excursions were beginning to fall, the remaining operators made attempts to lure trippers back on board by offering entertainment. This poster advertises the attractions offered on the Bournemouth-based paddle steamer *Embassy* owned by Cosens and Company of Weymouth. She was originally the *Duchess of Norfolk* employed on the Portsmouth to Ryde, Isle of Wight, railway ferry service and became the last operational steamer to operate from Bournemouth being withdrawn at the end of the 1966 excursion season.

September 1962 saw the end of an era when Cosens and Company of Weymouth withdrew the *Consul*, their last paddle steamer to ply from Weymouth. The company was unique in that they never owned or operated any other type of vessel than paddlers since the company was formed by Captain Joseph Cosens in 1852. Cosens continued to operate from Bournemouth until the end of the 1966 season with their last remaining vessel, the *Embassy*, and then withdrew from steamship ownership altogether.

This sailing bill shows the final Cosens sailings from Weymouth by *Consul* terminating on the 20th September, 1962.

SUSSEX QUEEN

The ex-*Freshwater* approaches Eastbourne Pier towards the end of her career on the 30th June, 1960. The 264 gross tons vessel was finally withdrawn from passenger service one year later.

WEYMOUTH, BOURNEMOUTH AND SWANAGE STEAM PACKET COMPANY
Steamers with Buff Funnels, Black Tops.

COSENS & CO., LIMITED. Established 1852. 'Phone No. 333. Telegraphic Address "Cosens, Weymouth."

STEAMER TRIPS

From WEYMOUTH HARBOUR PLEASURE PIER, weather, number of passengers, and other circumstances permitting

SUNDAY, SEPTEMBER 16th—H.W. 9.30 a.m. 9.46 p.m. B.S.T.

2 15 p.m. **CRUISE ROUND H.M. SHIPS AND MERCHANT SHIPPING IN PORTLAND HARBOUR** and a tour of the Roadstead. **Fare 4/-**

3 15 p.m. **TEA CRUISE TO THE BILL OF PORTLAND,** viewing Pennsylvania Cove and Castle, Lighthouse, Pulpit Rock, etc., due back 5.15 p.m. **Fare 7/-.** (Teas supplied at moderate charges).

MONDAY, SEPTEMBER 17th—H.W. 10.08 a.m., 10.29 p.m. B.S.T.

2 0 p.m. **CRUISE ROUND H.M. SHIPS AND MERCHANT SHIPPING IN PORTLAND HARBOUR.** **Fare 4/-**

3 0 p.m. **CRUISE** across Weymouth Bay, towards Osmington, Ringstead and Lulworth Cove thence to Portland Harbour viewing H.M. Ships and Merchant Shipping, due back 4.45 p.m. **Fare 7/-**

TUESDAY, SEPTEMBER 18th—H.W. 10.45 a.m., 11.11 p.m. B.S.T.

2 0 p.m. **CRUISE ROUND H.M. SHIPS AND MERCHANT SHIPPING IN PORTLAND HARBOUR** and a tour of the Roadstead. **Fare 4/-**

3 0 p.m. **TEA CRUISE TO THE SHAMBLES LIGHTSHIP** in the English Channel, due back 5 p.m. **Fare 7/-** (Teas supplied at moderate charges). Newspapers, Magazines, etc., are welcome aboard the Lightship.

7 30 p.m. **A GRAND ILLUMINATION CRUISE**
To view Weymouth's 'Fairylike' Illuminations from the best vantage point obtainable. The Steamer will proceed to Portland Harbour viewing H.M. Ships and Merchant Shipping, etc., thence towards Osmington and Ringstead and then across Weymouth Bay. A special commentary will be given upon points of interest en route. This is a trip you and your children must not miss. Due back about 9.0 p.m. **Special Cheap Fare 6/-**, Children half-price.

WEDNESDAY, SEPTEMBER 19th—H.W. 11.21 a.m., 11.48 p.m. B.S.T.

10 45 a.m. **COFFEE CRUISE** across Weymouth Bay, towards Osmington and Ringstead, thence to Portland Harbour viewing H.M. Ships and Merchant Shipping, due back 12.15 p.m. **Fare 6/6** (including Coffee)

2 0 p.m. **CRUISE ROUND H.M. SHIPS AND MERCHANT SHIPPING IN PORTLAND HARBOUR** and a tour of the Roadstead. **Fare 4/-**

3 0 p.m. **TEA CRUISE TO THE BILL OF PORTLAND** viewing Pennsylvania Cove and Castle, Lighthouse, Pulpit Rock, etc., due back 5 p.m. **Fare 7/-** (Teas supplied at moderate charges).

THURSDAY, SEPTEMBER 20th—H.W. 11.56 a.m. B.S.T.

2 0 p.m. **CRUISE ROUND H.M. SHIPS AND MERCHANT SHIPPING IN PORTLAND HARBOUR** and a tour of the Roadstead. **Fare 4/-**

3 0 p.m. **LULWORTH COVE.** Dorset's famous beauty spot, giving wonderful views of rugged coastal scenery en route, landing until 5 p.m., due back 6 p.m. **Fare 8/-**

End of Excursion Season

> **N.B. Re LULWORTH COVE TRIP**
> Should the weather be unfit for this, a cruise will be substituted commencing at 3.0 p.m
> (See Pier Booking Office Notice Board.)

THE STEAMER IS FULLY LICENSED. TEAS AND REFRESHMENTS SERVED ON BOARD

ADVANCE BOOKINGS. Tickets may be obtained in advance for the evening cruise from the Pier Steamer Booking Office each day from 1 to 4.30 p.m.

IMPORTANT NOTICE—CONDITIONS OF CARRIAGE

This photograph of the harbour at Weymouth taken on the 14th November, 1962, shows three paddle steamers each belonging to a different company. They are in descending order from the camera, *Consul* at that time belonging to Cosens of Weymouth, the White Funnel Fleet flagship *Bristol Queen* of P. and A. Campbell Ltd., and *Sandown* which operated the British Rail ferry between Portsmouth and the Isle of Wight.

Both the *Bristol Queen* and *Sandown* were at Weymouth receiving attention by engineers from Cosens. The *Consul* had a few weeks previously completed her final sailings for the same company.

CONSUL

This early morning scene at Weymouth shows the *Consul* of 1896 raising steam for the last time on the 4th February, 1965, prior to leaving for the River Dart where she was adapted to provide accommodation for yachting holidays.

QUEEN LINE STEAMERS

1963 SEASON SUMMER CRUISES

by p.s. "MEDWAY QUEEN"

Daily (except Fridays)

on the RIVER MEDWAY and THAMES ESTUARY

Until Sunday, 8th September, 1963

Every Saturday
TWO SAILINGS TO SOUTHEND

(NON-LANDING)

Depart STROOD	9.30 a.m.	4.15 p.m.
Arrive SOUTHEND	11.10 a.m.	5.55 p.m.
Depart SOUTHEND	11.30 a.m.	6.15 p.m.
Arrive STROOD	1.10 p.m.	7.55 p.m.

On 17th and 31st August

Depart STROOD 3.30 p.m.
Depart SOUTHEND 5.30 p.m.

Every Monday and Wednesday
TO SOUTHEND & CLACTON

Depart STROOD 9.15 a.m.
" SOUTHEND 11.00 a.m.
Arrive CLACTON 1.25 p.m.

Depart CLACTON 2.45 p.m.
(SEA TRIP)
Arrive CLACTON 4.15 p.m.

Depart CLACTON 4.25 p.m.
" SOUTHEND 6.40 p.m.
Arrive STROOD 8.40 p.m.

Every Sunday, Tuesday and Thursday
TO SOUTHEND & HERNE BAY

Depart STROOD 9.15 a.m.
" SOUTHEND 11.00 a.m.
" HERNE BAY 12.30 p.m.
Arrive SOUTHEND 2.15 p.m.

Depart SOUTHEND 3.15 p.m.
" HERNE BAY 5.00 p.m.
" SOUTHEND 6.40 p.m.
Arrive STROOD 8.40 p.m.

FARES FROM STROOD

TO			SINGLE		DAY RETURN	PERIOD
SOUTHEND	Sun., Mon., Tues., Wed. and Thurs.		7/-	approx. 7½ hrs. ashore	10/-	12/6
SOUTHEND	Saturdays (Non-Landing 7/6)			approx. 7 hrs. ashore	10/-	
HERNE BAY	Sundays, Tuesdays and Thursdays		7/6	approx. 4½ hrs. ashore	11/-	12/6
CLACTON	Mondays and Wednesdays		10/6	approx. 3 hrs. ashore	14/-	18/6
MARGATE (CHANGE AT SOUTHEND)	Daily (except Fridays and also 17th, 18th and 31st August)		12/-	approx. 2 hrs. ashore	15/-	20/-

Children under 14 half fare. Under 3 years free

Special Cruises on 17th & 31st August to view Southend Illuminations Departing Strood 7.30 p.m. 7/6

CATERING, REFRESHMENTS AND FULLY LICENSED BARS ON BOARD

Bicycles 5/- single.
No dogs allowed on board.

Luggage allowed to Single and Period Passengers only.
Passengers are carried only on the terms and conditions printed on the back of this handbill.
All Sailings are subject to weather and other circumstances permitting.
Tickets may be obtained in advance from

THE NEW MEDWAY STEAM PACKET CO. LTD.
Gas House Road, Rochester. Phone: Chatham 41355/6

MEDWAY TRAVEL BUREAU
44 High Street, Rochester
Phone: Chatham 44673
G.S. No. 2. 1963.

FEATHERSTONES LTD.
375 High Street, Rochester
Phone: Chatham 41414

PICKFORDS TRAVEL SERVICE
24 Railway Street, Chatham
Phone: Chatham 43453

"PATS"
346A High Street, Chatham
Phone: Chatham 42953

2003 BRIGHTON & SOUTH COAST STEAMERS LTD. 2003
Brighton to WORTHING
Fare as Advertised
Issued subject to conditions as stated in the Company's Time Tables and Bills.

2002 BRIGHTON & SOUTH COAST STEAMERS LTD. 2002
Brighton to WORTHING
Fare as Advertised
Issued subject to conditions as stated in the Company's Time Tables and Bills.

MEDWAY QUEEN

The *Medway Queen* turns at the start of another day's excursions to Southend or Herne Bay.

This signed sailing bill issued in September 1963 by the New Medway Steam Packet Company of Rochester shows the last regular trips on the River Medway and Thames Estuary by the paddle steamer *Medway Queen*. The programme was signed by members of her crew under the command of Captain L. Horsham during her last sailing to Southend and Herne Bay on Sunday, 8th September, 1963.

The *Medway Queen* built by the Ailsa Shipbuilding Company of Troon, Scotland, in 1924 served all her operational life under the same ownership except when impressed into naval service during the Second World War. During the evacuation of British troops from Dunkirk in May 1940 she evacuated over 7,000 troops during seven trips to the beach.

Her design was based on that of a similar Ailsa vessel constructed in 1908, that of the *Bournemouth Queen*. Both ships having full-length promenade decks that extended practically all the way from stern to stern. The *Medway Queen*'s paddle box was also of traditional design with thirteen openings to dissipate water in heavy seas. Her bridge was unusual in that it remained open without a wheelhouse, the Captain and helmsman being protected only by white canvas dodgers.

When withdrawn several attempts were made to preserve the vessel culminating in her being towed during 1964 to the River Medina in the Isle of Wight for use with a proposed yacht marina.

10 Restoration and Preservation

In Britain one of the first attempts to preserve a paddle steamer in a non-operational capacity was made with the *Alexandra*, which had seen service on the railway connection to the Isle of Wight and also as a unit of the Cosens fleet registered at Weymouth. In 1932, she was sold to Captain A. G. Hardie and converted for use on the Thames as a floating cabaret showboat, the English equivalent of an American showboat. She was re-decked and a theatre was erected over her saloon. The vessel was too small to attract the type of clientele required and in 1933, with her engines removed, she was moored off Margate, being later re-stationed near Shoreham. Success eluded her, however, and plans were made to move the vessel to the Manchester Ship Canal, but before the tow could be undertaken creditors moved in and the showboat *Alexandra* went instead to the breakers.

The paddle steamer *Lymington* was perhaps more successful. When withdrawn in 1929 she at first saw service as a houseboat and later as Sea Scout Headquarters ship in Norfolk.

Neither of these, however, were definite attempts at preservation and it was only after many suitable candidates for preservation had gone to the breakers that enthusiasts began to look at the remaining examples as worthy of saving.

By the 1960's it was clear that few of the remaining paddle steamers in Britain had any long expectancy of life. The first attempt by the Paddle Steamer Preservation Society to preserve the Pembroke-to-Neyland ferry *Alumchine* in 1963 met with failure, as the Society at that time was still in its infancy and did not possess the necessary personnel to undertake such a project. By 1965, however, when the *Medway Queen* was about to be scrapped the P.S.P.S. was in a position to arouse public opinion and interest, with the result that the ship was eventually purchased for use in a proposed marina on the River Medina near Cowes, Isle of Wight. Unfortunately, the marina was beset with difficulties and some years later the *Medway Queen* was in a poor condition. In 1978 attempts were still being made to save her.

As more and more ships were scrapped it was realised that the scarcity value of those remaining would increase. One of the more successful attempts at preservation in a static rôle has been that of the ex-Clyde paddle *Caledonia*, now the *Old Caledonia* moored near Waterloo Bridge in London and operated in a very efficient manner by the Brewers, Bass Charrington, as a floating restaurant and bar.

Close by are the *Tattershall Castle*, an ex-Humber ferry which serves as an art gallery and conference centre, and the *Princess Elizabeth*, in service as another restaurant and bar. Both these vessels are under private ownership and are good examples of the use to which this type of vessel can be adapted. It is perhaps surprising that Scotland, the birthplace of the paddle steamer, has no static example moored on her waters and the National Maritime Museum at Greenwich has shown little interest in preserving an example of the once numerous British excursion steamers, although it is to their credit that they have preserved the ex-tug *John H. Amos* in a static capacity.

The preservation of a paddle steamer is of course beset with difficulty, the sheer economics of maintaining an old vessel subject to corrosion by weather and water being enormous. Whilst static preservation is better than nothing, it is the operational use of a paddle steamer that fulfills the main ambition of the preservationist. If the difficulties of static preservation are enormous, then operational preservation is almost financially unsurmountable, unless grants, subsidies and revenue from sponsors are readily obtainable. To this effect, we must commend the efforts of the Waverley Steam Navigation Company in their tireless attempts to maintain in an operational rôle the world's last sea-going excursion paddle steamer *Waverley*.

In Europe, a number of lake and river steamers are still afloat and in use as static restaurants, such as the *Neuchatel* of 1912 and *Fribourg*, 1913, on Lake Neuchatel and the Dutch *Reederij Op de Leh 2* of 1895, moored on the Rhine at Andernach. Other ex-steamers have been converted to headquarters for yachting clubs and centres, whilst we must not forget the former Swiss paddler *Rigi* of 1848, now happily preserved as the centrepiece of the Swiss Transport Museum at Lucerne. In America, following in the wake of the mighty San Francisco Bay ferries, the little tug *Eppleton Hall*, which crossed the Atlantic entirely under her own power in 1969-70, is still seaworthy, having her own fan club, the Friends of the *Eppleton Hall*, to ensure that she remains on the active list and meets the safety requirements of the U.S. Coast Guards. Both the *Eppleton Hall* and the now static Bay ferry *Eureka* are important units of the San Francisco Maritime Museum, which has done so much to preserve examples of maritime history.

It is unfortunate that there are no examples of the paddle liner or paddle cross-channel steamer left to preserve, but such is the interest now shown in the remaining coastal, lake and river steamers, that some examples at least are bound to become subjects for preservation. Europe would appear to be the last operational paddle steamer arena, its re-engined and rebuilt examples continuing in service for some years to come. Already the remaining operators are realising the vintage attraction that their steamers are creating. In 1977, for example, the Köln-Dusseldorfer Deutsche Rheinschiffahrt restyled the paddle-boxes of their vessels in an attempt to make them more easily recognisable as paddlers, a sign perhaps that the paddler has won a place in men's hearts as well as a place in maritime history.

ALUMCHINE

This small paddler of some 76 gross tons became the first candidate for preservation in 1962 by the then newly formed Paddle Steamer Preservation Society. She had been originally constructed in 1923 for the Caernarvon to Foel in Anglesey ferry service, but ten years later was purchased for a similar service between Pembroke and Neyland. In the autumn of 1962 the P.S.P.S. made strenuous efforts to retain the vessel for further use from Southampton. Membership however was insufficient to raise sufficient funds to purchase and tow the steamer to the South coast and the *Alumchine* was eventually scrapped in 1965.

COMPTON CASTLE

The ornate paddle box of the ex-River Dart river steamer *Compton Castle*, preserved as a restaurant at Kingsbridge, Devon, where she has served in this rôle since 1964.

GEM

The Australian paddler *Gem* has been superseded as a pleasure steamer and withdrawn from passenger service. The *Gem* is seen here in her new capacity as part of the Swan Hill Folk Museum in South Australia.

MARION

Once a typical example of an Australian river paddler, the *Marion* has now been happily preserved and is moored at the side of the river upon which she used to ply. This triple-decked wooden steamer is now a museum and tourist attraction at the town of Mannum on the River Murray.

RIGI

Rigi's maiden voyage took place on the 1st April, 1848, and after minor adjustments she entered regular service on the lake from the 30th May. After forty-six years of service her engine was replaced by Escher-Wyss Ltd. of Zurich and in 1872 her boiler was changed for one of higher pressure in an attempt to increase her original speed of 12 knots.

The *Rigi* remained in continuous summer service until after the 1952 season, apart from the years 1916–19 when she laid up because the First World War had brought about a decline in the number of tourists and passengers on the Swiss lakes. It was estimated that during her one hundred and five years of service the *Rigi* had steamed a distance the equivalent of thirty times around the globe and had carried more than 6 million passengers. When withdrawn the *Rigi* was donated to the Swiss Museum of Transport and Communications where she is now used as a restaurant.

The 1848 *Rigi* is seen here whilst still in service as a passenger steamer in 1948.

RIGI

Now an important exhibit at the Swiss Museum of Transport and Communications situated at Lucerne, the paddle steamer *Rigi* (originally spelt *Righi*) served one hundred and five years in the service for which she was built.

The *Rigi* was constructed by Ditchburn and Marc of London for the Mail Steamship Company of Lake Lucerne in 1847 (Postdamfschiffahrtgesellschaft auf dem Vierwaldstättersee). Engined with oscillating machinery by John Penn and Sons, the vessel was moved by water from London to Strasbourg. From there the 90-ton vessel was transported by rail to Basle, being partially dismantled for this stage of her journey. Finally horses were used to bring the vessel to Lake Lucerne where she was reassembled by British workers.

CALEDONIA

The Clyde steamer *Caledonia* is seen here during overhaul at Lamont's yard, Port Glasgow, in March 1962. Operated by the Caledonia Steam Packet Company and built in 1934, during the Second World War she saw service under the name of *H.M.S. Goatfell* as a minesweeper and anti-aircraft vessel as well as taking part in the Normandy invasion in June 1944.

Returning to passenger service in May 1946 under her original name, and employed on summer excursions, she made her final run on the 7th October, 1969, before being offered for sale. Two years later the 624 gross tons vessel was acquired by Charringtons and work began on conversion to a floating pub and restaurant. A conversion which happily has retained the character of the vessel.

PRINCESS ELIZABETH

The last paddle steamer owned by the Southampton, Isle of Wight and South of England Royal Mail Steam Packet Company is now owned by James Lynch (Inns) Limited of London and moored close to Tower Bridge where the 1927 vessel is in use as a restaurant and bar. Pictured here on a damp cold morning in February 1978 the *Lizzie* awaits the brighter days of spring and summer, in order to cater for the tourist trade to the British capital, although she is open each evening throughout the year to Thames-siders and visitors.

OLD CALEDONIA
The former Clyde paddle steamer *Caledonia* now tied up at a permanent mooring near Waterloo Bridge presents a striking sight to visitors and Londoners at night in her new capacity as a restaurant.

OLD CALEDONIA
The magnificent triple diagonal engines of the *Caledonia* are preserved in their ▶ original condition although their hissing steam and smell of lubricating oil have gone for ever.

WAVERLEY

Whilst representative examples of lake and river paddle steamers are likely to remain in operation for some time to come, especially those converted from steam to other forms of propulsion, the honour of being the world's last sea-going paddle steamer has befallen the *Waverley*, formerly a member of the railway-controlled Clyde paddler fleet.

The 693 gross tons *Waverley* was built in 1947 by A. and J. Inglis Ltd. of Glasgow. She is fitted with a fine example of oil-fired triple-expansion engines capable of propelling the twin-funnelled vessel at a speed of 17 knots. She replaced a vessel of the same name sunk at Dunkirk.

Her maiden voyage took place on the 16th June, 1947, on a cruise up Loch Goil and Loch Long to Lochgoilhear and Arrochar. During her first season she wore the colours of the London and North Eastern Railway Company but upon the absorption of that concern into the British Transport Commission, her attractive red, white and black-topped funnels adopted the less exciting pale yellow and black of the Commission's shipping subsidiary, the Caledonian Steam Packet Company. In 1973 she was transferred to the newly formed Caledonian McBrayne Ltd. Her last season as a regular excursion steamer on the Clyde under this ownership was in 1973 when many thought that the age of paddle propulsion on the Clyde had reached its final stage.

Following representations made by the British Paddle Steamer Preservation Society to Caledonian McBrayne, a meeting was held in January 1974 to discuss the future of the vessel, the meeting being attended by representatives of various tourist boards. Prior to this meeting *Waverley*'s owners had offered the ship to the Paddle Steamer Preservation Society for the sum of £1, no doubt hoping that their last operational paddle steamer would be a worthy candidate for preservation.

Further discussions and meetings took place whilst the vessel was laid up during 1974 and a new company, The Waverley Steam Navigation Co. Ltd., was formed by the P.S.P.S. to look after the affairs of the vessel. On the 8th August, 1974, she was officially handed over, Sir Patrick Thomas, Chairman of the Scottish Transport Group donating the £1 to meet this extraordinary selling price.

Waverley Steam Navigation had made no secret of the fact that preservation meant operation and through dint of considerable hard work, grants were obtained from a number of sources towards her renovation. Many commercial concerns offered help and a public appeal was launched to help raise funds.

As a result of all this effort, on the 10th May, 1975, her fires were relit and four days later *Waverley* sailed for the first time for 20 months into the waters of the Clyde. Since then the vessel has operated successfully for her new and enthusiastic owners sponsored by the Preservation Society and it is to be hoped that this last remaining example of a sea-going paddle steamer will be run successfully for many seasons to come.

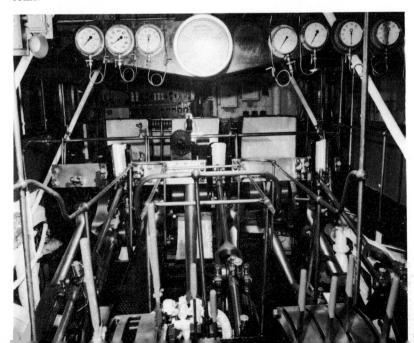

Bibliography

Admiral Sir Reginald Bacon	*The Dover Patrol*	Hutchinson
G. Body	*British Paddle Steamers*	David and Charles
F. Burtt	*Cross-Channel and Coastal Paddle Steamers 1934*	Tilling
F. Burtt	*Steamers of the Thames and Medway*	Tilling
R. H. Cotton	*A Decline of the Paddle Steamer*	P.S.P.S. Publication
F. Dittmar and J. Colledge	*British Warships 1914–19*	Ian Allan
C. Duckworth and G. Langmuir	*Clyde River and Other Steamers*	Brown, Son and Ferguson
C. Duckworth and G. Langmuir	*Railway and Other Steamers*	Shipping Histories Ltd.
B. Dumpleton	*The Story of the Paddle Steamer*	Colin Venton
G. Farr	*West Country Passenger Steamers*	Stephenson
J. Grigsby	*Royal Yachts 1604–1953*	Adlard Coles
J. Guthrie	*Bizarre Ships of the Nineteenth Century*	Hutchinson
F. C. Hambleton	*Famous Paddle Steamers 1948*	Marshall
F. G. MacHaffie	*Waverley*	Waverley S.N. Company
A. McQueen	*Echoes of Old Clyde Paddle Wheels*	Gowans and Gray
I. Mudie	*River Boats*	Rigby
F. T. O'Brien	*Early Solent Steamers*	David and Charles
G. W. O'Connor	*The First Hundred Years*	Camelot Press
R. Plummer	*Paddle Steamers in the 70's*	Anglia County Press
M. H. Spies	*Veteran Steamers*	Spies (Denmark)
F. Thornley	*Steamers of North Wales*	Stephenson
E. Thornton	*South Coast Pleasure Steamers*	Stephenson

Index of Vessels

Wherever possible the original date of construction has been given although the vessel may have sailed under other names on a later occasion. Where the date of launch has not been readily available the prefix 'c' denotes the approximate date of entering service. Italics refer to illustrations.

Acknowledgements. The author and publishers gratefully acknowledge the following for their help in providing illustrations and for permission to reproduce them in this book: Bristol City Museum; British Rail; Robert W. Brookes; F. Burtt; The Delta Queen Steam Co., David Couling; German Democratic Republic Tourist Agency; General Steam Navigation Co.; Grangemouth Towing Ltd.; F. W. Hawkes; Charrington & Co.; Imperial War Museum, London; Italian State Tourist Office; J. Jackson; M. Lindenborn; J. M. Mallinson; National Library of Ireland; Origination Photo & Picture Library, Bournemouth; Paddle Steamer Preservation Society; R. A. Plummer; Red Funnel Steamers: San Francisco Maritime Museum, Dr. Ernst Schmidt; The Science Museum, London; Basil Sexton; South Australian Govt. Publicity and Tourist Bureau; Steamship Historical Society of America; Waverley Steam Navigation Co. The author also acknowledges his indebtness for kind help and information supplied by: The Royal Norwegian Embassy, London; New Zealand High Commission, London; Richard Braun; Jan Lodder; Richard Clammer. The publishers would also like to thank Hutchinson's for permission to quote from their book 'The Dover Patrol' by Admiral Sir Reginald Bacon and John Murray (publishers) Ltd for permission to quote from 'Excursion to Hell' by J. B. Priestley.